Bullying and Young Children

What is it that makes some children bully and some become victims?

What can you do if, despite your best efforts, one child keeps on taunting another?

What steps can you take before communicating with parents and what will you say?

The practice of bullying en hools today. Despite the implementation of policie on b and n be equally perplexed, no ally und stan v en't done to allow it to hap en.

Christine acintyre e es th emotive answering many frequently asked questions and exploring why as many as one in twelve school children are victims of bullying. She examines the roots of the problem, looking at bullying from the earliest ages.

This highly practical book shows practitioners what can be done to support the children and to help them improve their own practice, providing help and guidance on:

- enhancing the self-esteem of the affected children, showing how new-found confidence will enable children to offset the effects of being bullied or indeed being a bully;
- how to tell parents their child is bullying or being bullied, and how to build up a meaningful and mutually supportive relationship with them;
- creating a learning environment that prevents the desire for children to bully.

Based on case studies giving first-hand accounts of real-life situations, and evaluations of strategies that have been tried and tested, this book suggests fresh and inspiring ways of tackling a problem faced by many practitioners today.

Christine Macintyre is an Educational Consultant and prolific author, formerly at the Moray House Institute, University of Edinburgh.

Bullying and Young Children

Understanding the issues and tackling the problem

Christine Macintyre

Routledge
Taylor & Francis Group

LONDON AND NEW YORK

First published 2009
by Routledge
2 Park Square, Milton Park, Abingdon, Oxon OX14 4RN

Simultaneously published in the USA and Canada
by Routledge
270 Madison Avenue, New York, NY 10016

Routledge is an imprint of the Taylor & Francis Group

Text © 2009 Christine Macintyre
Illustrations in text © 2009 David Barrington

Typeset in Palatino by
Keystroke, 28 High Street, Tettenhall, Wolverhampton
Printed and bound in Great Britain by
MPG Books Group, UK

British Library Cataloguing in Publication Data
A catalogue record for this book is available from the British Library

Library of Congress Cataloging in Publication Data
MacIntyre, Christine, 1938–
Bullying & young children : understanding the issues and tackling the
problem / Christine Macintyre.
p. cm.
Includes bibliographical references and index.
1. Bullying in schools. I. Title. II. Title: Bullying and young children.
LB3013.3.M243 2009
371.5'8—dc22   2008047538

ISBN 10: 0–415–48496–0 (pbk)
ISBN 13: 978–0–415–48496–1 (pbk)

Contents

Acknowledgements

There are many people who have made this book possible and I should like to thank them all. First, my thanks to the children who brought their role -playing activities to fruition through writing the poems that appear throughout the text. These youngsters developed them in a creative writing lesson to heighten their awareness of bullying issues. This had begun as an activity to develop empathy through understanding the feelings of both bullies and victims. In the process they came to appreciate the very different reasons that influenced them to behave in this way. Thank you too to their teacher for leading them in this creative endeavour. Another group of young people designed the posters to illustrate the points they had learned during their anti-bullying week. They displayed these in a local supermarket where they raised awareness in children who had not had such an opportunity.

Thank you too to the experienced professionals who shared their strategies for coping with bullying incidents and communicating distressing news to parents. Often they were perplexed that despite all their efforts, bullying had not totally disappeared, but encouraged by some successes they vowed to keep trying different strategies and sharing their concerns. They hope that their experiences will enable others to see that they are not alone in trying to stamp out the scourge that is bullying.

And a huge thank you to Lucy Wainwright at Routledge and the team at Keystroke for the professional production of the text.

My thanks especially go to David Barrington who has captured the feeling of the poems in his drawings.

Everyone hopes that children will live in harmony without bullying, so that they may enjoy their childhood without the fear and oppression that bullying brings. It is vital that they do, for after all, 'it is to the young that the future belongs'.

Introduction

'Why are you sad?' they asked me.
'Why are you sad all day?'
'I'm sad because these other
children never let me play!'

'You said to ask them nicely,
I did but they ran away
and said if I told they'd hit me.
They really spoil my day.'

If parents were allowed only one wish for their children at school, I am sure it would be that their young people would be happy there. But of course this is a complex ideal. What do they mean? Probably that their children should be healthy and develop the confidence to make friends, and the abilities and skills to allow them to participate in all aspects of the curriculum with enjoyment and some success. This seems an entirely reasonable hope, yet sinister events like bullying can spoil children's schooldays, even their life chances. The negative effects of bullying can be devastating and for some children endure for many years after leaving school and those who persecuted them there. They can even result in adults having difficulty trusting friends, which can lead to isolation and strained relationships (Alexander *et al.* 2004a, b). Many if not all schools have anti-bullying policies now, yet despite these, 27 per cent of our primary-age children report that they have been 'the victim of systematic sustained hostility from a group of peers who consistently made their lives hell' (Thornton 2007). There is no doubt that the problem still persists.

Imagine what it is like to have your child distressed day after day, frightened to go to school, coming home in tears but seemingly unwilling or unable to explain why. What can you do? 'Hoping it will go away' is not a useful strategy, yet many parents, perhaps afraid their child has done something to merit being bullied, or not just knowing how to confront the issue, feel too inhibited to do more. Or perhaps they fear, or have heard whispers, that their own child is a bully. How chilling is that? There may be no obvious reason why their child has started bullying, or perhaps they suspect that the bullying has sprung up as a survival mechanism in retaliation for someone else's unacceptable behaviour. On the other hand, parents may recognise that their child is a bully because they have met his hostile and consistently aggressive behaviour at home. They may wonder if there is a neurological cause, because their child won't listen to reason and 'only seems elated when he's causing mayhem' (distracted mum who 'has tried everything'). Alternatively, parents may blame each other, citing genetic reasons, for example 'He's turning out just like your father. He was loud and wouldn't listen to reason.' Recriminations like this can cause the problem to spiral out of control. What can, or should, parents do?

And if or when parents of children who are victims of bullying decide to go to school to 'get to the bottom of it all', and the child begs them to stay at home 'because you will only make things worse', what then? Should they override their child's pleas? Despite the ethos of schools building positive relationships with parents, facing up to discussing an emotive issue like bullying with someone who is a relative stranger is very hard. Perhaps this is why only 4 per cent of parents do so (Byrne 2003).

And when does bullying begin? Is there a cut-off time when the strategies toddlers sometimes use, such as shoving and biting, change from being recognised as unacceptable passing phases to being bullying behaviours? Can one really accept that babies are born bullies? With more and more children entering childcare venues for longer spells, this is a serious question that must be investigated. Children cannot be left vulnerable to harm.

And so this book explains what bullying is and why, despite the best efforts of parents and school personnel, it endures. It seeks to reassure parents of both victims and bullies that they and their children are not alone, and it suggests ways to make changes in understandings, models and actions so that all children learn better ways of coping. Many children bully in a mistaken effort to gain status; some undeserving children are picked on for trivial reasons or for no reason at all. Some children can express their real or unfounded worries at school yet cannot talk about them at home – or the opposite scenario can exist. And some potential victims join the bullies as a survival mechanism, afraid that if they do not adopt what they know in their hearts is unacceptable behaviour, they will be targeted next. And sadly some children appear to enjoy bullying. They appear deaf to entreaties to desist; they are not abashed by explanations that if they continue with bullying tactics, no one will want them for a friend. Even the threat of sanctions and exclusion can leave some children unmoved. One 10-year-old, reminded about the possibility of exclusion, retorted, 'I don't want to be in your school anyway' (adjectives missed out!). There are a myriad of occurrences that leave onlookers aghast.

No matter the stimulus or the response, however, there must be things that can be done. The most bullying action of all would be to stand aside and do nothing. Unfortunately, there is not one infallible strategy that will work in all situations. The children's difficulties need to be understood in context and then the most appropriate strategies for each situation need to be selected and tried. There is neither one 'typical bully' who does certain things, nor one 'typical victim' who reacts in an expected way. Identification and remediation would be much simpler if that were the case. This is what makes gathering evidence and recording occurrences of bullying so hard. Incidents can appear trivial in the retelling yet have profoundly unhappy effects. How can a sly leer or a sudden threatening silence be quantified, far less be proved? Yet these strategies can cause as much pain as a physical assault. And of course bullies usually choose times to inflict pain when no onlookers are present. 'Bullying is most often a secret affair' (Thornton 2007).

While many children are bullied for any reason or for no reason at all, it is sad that some who already have to cope with additional support needs are particularly susceptible to being targeted. Being different in any way, such as in developmental status, in ethnicity, or even having to wear spectacles, can make children vulnerable. It is especially sad that children who already have to cope with learning differences and disabilities are often, even usually, targeted by bullies. Talking of her two sons with autism, Charlotte Moore (2004) is sure that 'They *will* be bullied, it's par for the course' – and this in a culture that urges us to foster inclusion and to appreciate and celebrate differences. Explanations of some learning differences or difficulties and indicators that are often 'picked on' come throughout the book, but particularly in Chapter 2.

Then, as confident, outgoing children – that is, those with high self-esteem – are less likely to be either bullies or victims, Chapters 5 and 6 explain the intricate nature of bullying and suggest ways in which the self-esteem of children who lack confidence may be enhanced. Many children need help to become more assertive and they need to appreciate the subtle difference between that and aggressive behaviour. They need both verbal and non-verbal strategies that enable them to defeat the bullies and a positive outlook that tells the bullies they will be overcome.

Throughout the text, examples of teachers' and children's work illustrate activities that have been designed specifically to reduce all kinds of bullying. Then in Chapter 6 come practical strategies that can be tried and evaluated in different settings.

So, how can we tackle bullying? We certainly can't give up! Let's start at the beginning and ask questions about bullying in the earliest years, then venture into primary-age classrooms and share some of the work being carried out in Edinburgh schools. The aim is for home and school, preferably working together, to provide the children with reassurance and positive proof that all caring adults have a single aim: to protect all children from the scourge that bullying is.

One of the most worrying traits is the huge rise in sexual bullying. The Department for Children, Schools and Families (DCSF) claim that 3,500 pupils were suspended for sexual bullying in one year in England alone, and 260 of these were still at primary school. In fact 20 children were just five years old. So name-calling has taken on a new, sinister dimension. What sorts of occurrences go under this heading? The charity Beatbullying lists sexual misconduct, e.g. explicit graffiti, name-calling and inappropriate touching and even serious assaults such as being forced to participate in sex acts.

Why does this happen? Michelle Elliot from Kidscape explains that 'sexual bullying has almost become a way of asserting your power over others and for that reason it is disturbing'. The DCSF are due to publish guidelines on dealing with it in 2009. A national database to monitor the scale of the problem is to be set up. At the moment parents can be alarmed by the lack of immediate appropriate response from schools. But of course many instances are hidden and it is so difficult for children to share their ordeals. As with all bullying, the first step staff must take is to let the perpetrators know that their acts will be recorded, even reported to the police; that every incident will be taken seriously and time will be given to ensuring it is wiped out.

And of course staff can be the target of such bullying behaviour too, e.g. leering and cat calling. Pupils can even post sexually explicit comments on the internet and 'many female pupils face the same appalling behaviour' (Keats, National Secretary NASUWT).

Let us hope that if we can stamp out bullying in the Early Years, it will not emerge later on. The damage to the young victims and the bullies is devastating and long lasting. Somehow children must learn to empathise with others and not be so stressed that they react in this aggressive, sexual, totally unacceptable way.

1 Twenty questions about bullying

A big black cloud is choking me,
My throat is tight and sore,
I don't want to go to this school
Any more.

Ashleigh, aged 9

Question 1: Do very young children bully?

The question of whether very young children can be said to bully is not an easy one. If the answer is 'yes', – and both school exclusion reports for 4-year-olds and many early years practitioners have no doubt that this is the case – what sorts of things do they do and why do they do it? And if the answer is 'no', then what causes some of them to start (for despite everyone's efforts to stop bullying, it is still endemic across social groups and occurs at all ages)? And what are the implications for the bullies, their victims and the families of both? No one will be surprised to learn that bullying 'is a precursor for health problems' or that such behaviour 'is an issue of major concern to children, their teachers and their parents' (Bond *et al.* 2001). So, observations of children's interactions and their understandings of the kinds of behaviour that are unacceptable need to be developed from children's earliest days.

Let's begin by reflecting on the children who come into our early years settings and on the experiences they encounter there.

Question 2: Who are the children?

The children are a group of very young people of different ages (and remember that one year can mean one-third of a child's life span) and different developmental stages (some of the 3-year-olds may be more able than the 4-year-olds), different shapes, sizes, ethnicity, intellectual abilities, social competences, movement skills and emotional stability. They have different capacities to understand and to use expressive language to share their needs, and there are differences in the languages and the dialects they use. Some learn with ease while others struggle to progress. Furthermore, there are easygoing children, confident and creative children alongside those who are acutely anxious or withdrawn. There are children who are slow to warm up and those that will not or cannot wait. These temperamental differences impact on their willingness to interact with others in their group and their motivation to learn. The children have hugely varied home and out-of-school experiences, levels of common sense and cultural beliefs. There are streetwise children who know their rights and are not afraid to proclaim them amid those who have been overly sheltered at home – and all shades in between. There are children with learning differences and difficulties, including the increasing number of children found to be on the autistic spectrum. These children have difficulty in understanding the thoughts and feelings of others, and so building relationships is hard. There are children with physical disabilities such as cerebral palsy who need extra support and children with attention deficit disorders who unwittingly may disturb the class. There are children who resent coming to school at all and vent their frustration on others, usually the more vulnerable ones. Is it any wonder that when we group all of them together in a confined space for a considerable length of time, some, possibly attempting to gain status and make themselves heard, resort to bullying?

To add to the complexity, interest and challenge of managing the children, they are not passive learners only waiting to hear parents' and practitioners' words of wisdom and advice. They come into a new situation with different expectations of what will be there, how important it will be and how they will cope. Some have neighbourhood friends to ease them into the setting, while others have none. They have radically different experiences of being parented; they have learned different 'rules', including rules about whether to retaliate when they are upset, and how to do it; how to look after resources; whether it is their job to tidy up; how to react when another adult tells them what to do; even what kinds of food they should have at snack. The differences between home rules and nursery or school rules can be very confusing. The children also have different levels of financial backing and opportunities to do exciting or challenging things, and varied amounts of home resources and parental support; and to some extent this colours their perception of what their future holds (Winston 2004). For as children develop self-awareness, they also begin to make comparisons between their lot and that of others. Real or even imagined unfairness can cause simmering resentments and feelings of low self-esteem.

Question 3: Could the early years setting possibly contribute to bullying?

All of these differences in individual children are brought together in a setting that is very different from home. It is certainly very busy, with many more experienced children appearing confident and totally in control of their learning and their friendships. For the new entrant, this can be comforting or daunting. The environment itself may be frightening, for example with toilets that flush noisily. One setting, proud of its new self-flushing loos, was dismayed that no child would go in. The reason? One child had suggested that a ghost was flushing them! Was that teasing or bullying or just fun? Maybe the answer depends on the effect of the delay! Then there are cookers behind barriers; bells that ring and radiators that buzz; walls that are covered by brightly coloured, confusing pictures; lights that flicker; and doors that have double locks. 'Who needs to be kept out?' asked one fearful child. Even the large floor space can be off-putting, especially if this encourages children to rush around.

And, of course, children have to meet new staff and learn new rules as well as tackle a whole range of new learning activities.

Question 4: What things do the children have to learn?

- That they will be safe without their parents or carers
- That their parents or carers will return
- How to follow a complex routine
- How to make a friend
- How to wait for a turn
- How to empathise with others
- How to deal with praise and rewards
- How to relate to 'strange' adults and other children who may not behave the way they do
- How to be still and listen to others
- How to share toys and resources
- How to climb on the frame and ride a bike outside

- How to make choices and decide what to do
- How to cut out distractions and concentrate
- How to do all the activities and tasks.

In their longitudinal study of children in Irish schools, Murray and Keane (1998) claim that 'those who cannot negotiate these early tasks are more likely to be bullied during their school lives'. Labels such as 'stupid' can persist well beyond the time when they applied by thoughtless, unsympathetic children. And this can happen in any environment. One eager 5-year-old was so anxious to enjoy his first swimming lesson that he stripped off and appeared at the poolside minus trunks! Years later he was still known as 'Hugh, you know, the boy who went swimming without his trunks on!' This shows how long poor Hugh had to endure chortles. Hugh considered this bullying, as he was extremely anxious to jettison the adjoinder but didn't know how. This longevity of early impressions is a very important claim and a huge endorsement for the value of early years education that places children's total well-being at the centre. Caring practitioners help erode embarrassments and decry labels that are not helpful.

The claim also has the implicit suggestion that, as many of the groups will stay together in the primary years, children may continue to categorise others by their initial inadequacies. Furthermore, these assessments may last over time, even when early difficulties have been overcome. So, what can practitioners do to ensure that negative labels do not stick?

Respecting differences

Above all, the children have to learn to respect themselves and the other children in the setting, the adults who care for them and the resources that are provided. They have to come to recognise that 'difference' is just that. It doesn't mean better or worse! The length of time this recognition takes will vary depending on the willingness of the child to settle, the coherence or conflict between the child's previous experiences and this new one, and of course the perceived attitudes of significant people such as teachers, nursery practitioners, janitors, dinner and playground personnel, and other children's parents in the environment. Indeed, this message is best passed on by example by the role models in the setting. However, if children do not learn by osmosis, then explanations have to be made, for perhaps no one has explained that certain ways of behaving could be named bullying. Sometimes we take it for granted that children understand when they have not yet developed the empathy or the experience to allow them to do so.

One shelter from being overwhelmed by all these demands is that most children of this age are egocentric (Piaget 1954). This term means that they tend to be tied up in their own existence and less aware of others in the setting. They gauge their new experiences in relation to the ones they have at home. Piaget's theory, based on minutely detailed observations of his own children, is confirmed by the developmental and cross-cultural stages of children's play. For all children practise solitary play, then experience parallel play, and this always precedes playing together in small then larger groups. Egocentricity can also be seen when children bring family photos into the setting and expect staff to know the names and relationships of people who are there, even the name of the family cat! Being like this should give children time to establish themselves in their new environment before they have a greater level of interaction with others and make possibly negative comparisons. But there is a paradox in that as children, at around 3 or 4 years of age, begin to understand that other people have different feelings and motives, this realisation may stimulate competition or bullying. So, it is vital that children have all the support they need in these early days because their developing self-awareness can impact cruelly on their self-esteem. This is why early positive feedback is so vital and why early compensatory programmes try to give needy children a boost before they self-evaluate and realise that others are ahead.

Fortunately, in a play-based curriculum the children can to a large extent choose what they want to do. This means that they can select activities at the level that matches their interests and their stage of development, or they can be imaginative and innovative, resulting in a learning process that should be free from stress. They can play alone or with just one friend till they gain the confidence and competence to join others in their game. Above all, there is time – not 'valuable time' (i.e. not-to-be-wasted time, full of hassle to get on), but time to listen and watch and grow. Even time to stand and stare!

In nursery, pre-school and school settings, young children have the positive role models provided by the staff, and in these settings they are immersed in an ethos that values all children equally. Yet despite practitioners claiming that they step in to avert unacceptable behaviour, still bullying behaviour – that is, persistent, intentional, conscious cruelty, perpetrated against those who are unable to defend themselves – survives.

Question 5: What sorts of behaviour could be called bullying?

Often researchers differentiate between teasing and bullying by the frequency of its occurrence. Byrne (2003) explains that 'bullying is a repetitive type of behaviour, not a one-off, transient occurrence'. This subsumes that it consists of premeditated actions and may explain why practitioners are reluctant to call early years' children bullies. Their actions, though just as hurtful, may be spur-of-the-moment actions carried out impetuously. He claims that 'there will always be name calling, slagging and teasing' but also warns that there is a line that should not be crossed. The trouble is delineating that line – does this not depend on the feelings of the child who is receiving the slurs or the slaps? Perhaps a more sympathetic approach would be to consider how the teased or bullied child is affected and name the effect by significance, not repetition? For even one incident can cause sensitive children to be nervous and worried through anticipating that it will happen again.

Question 6: What sorts of things can staff do?

Listen to some nursery practitioners. Nursery nurse Ann explains:

> You really need eyes in the back of your head in the nursery because incidents can flare up so quickly. If two children are having a spat about a toy, we jump in and praise: 'Aren't you a good boy to share so kindly? You must feel really good.' That can often defuse the situation and we hope that the children will reflect on the outcome, especially if we go on to provide something interesting for the one who has been prepared to wait.

So, Ann preferred to intervene, stressing the positive and through introducing a different activity made sure the child who complied didn't miss out.

Agreeing with this, her colleague Freya added:

> When this happens no one feels they have lost out, so the incident is over quickly. There's no lingering resentment in the younger age groups. Generally they just move on. Sometimes we see sulky faces and can feel resentment in the air, but generally we can suggest a song or a story and the moment passes. That's what's so good about the nursery curriculum; it can adapt to what's

going on and avoid blowing things out of proportion or nursing grievances.

In a slightly older setting with 6-year-olds, Jo vehemently disagreed:

> Being too subtle is just non-productive. If you prepare a lesson, perhaps using puppets to show how the bullied person feels, the children know fine what you are on about. They know the bullies in the group, but many of those who do persecute the others either don't listen or don't think it applies to them. I don't think this kind of approach helps the victims either. These children don't want to be seen as the underdog, the one who can't cope, i.e. the one everyone is sorry for. And some innocent ones wonder and worry if you are referring to them.
>
> It's much better to be upfront and not pussyfoot around. So I lay down the law. I tell the children, 'These are my rules – break them at your peril.' I tell them with a smile but they know I mean what I say. Then the children appreciate the boundaries and they feel safe. I make sure they all know the rules, and then if there is a tussle or any suggestion of bullying, I say 'excuse me' . . . and wait . . . and point to the list of rules – and the moment passes. Children need security like this!

In her pre-school class, Kiera puts a large notice on the main wall. It says 'We are all friends here and everyone gets to play' and the words are surrounded by examples of children's drawings. She explains:

> The younger children can't really read the words but we gather round every day and say it in unison. Then when I see a child welcoming a shy child into a game, he or she can put one of their drawings on the wall beside the poster. I hope the children will look at the drawings and remember the kind actions they represent. I think that really works.

Liam sets out to give his 5-year-olds choices and so promotes decision making and problem solving. He explained:

> When I see a tussle I try to set out different ways of doing things. For example, there were two boys coming to blows over whose turn it was to go on the bike. So I asked them both to calm down and then gave them alternatives. 'If you carry on fighting,' I explained, 'you'll both get hurt and the time for riding the bike

will be gone. Neither of you will get a turn. Is that a good idea? What else could we do?' Sometimes the children come up with ideas, or you have to be ready yourself – for example, 'If I set the big egg timer for Jack's turn and then I make sure you get the same length of time, will that do?' So in a way I leave the choice to them, and if I can, I ask them after the event if that worked well. If they say it did, I try to explain that there are always ways that are better than fighting. One day we saw two blackbirds chasing each other in the garden while a robin nipped in and took the food. I asked them if the birds reminded them of anyone and they nodded and smiled!

(See Chapter 6 for the poem 'Two Little Kittens', which illustrates this beautifully.)

Liam explained that another idea came to him when twins were squabbling over who had the bigger piece of apple at snack. The solution was to let one twin divide the apple and the other to choose which piece he should have! The outcome? 'You have never seen an apple divided so equally.' So, helping children to visualise alternative, better ways of doing things could reduce bullying, but the practitioner needs time to learn this strategy, and both parties have to agree that the solution is fair.

Thus, four very different strategies show that different staff, possibly through trial and error in different contexts, find their own best way.

Question 7: Are some children more likely to be bullied than others?

Foundation-stage practitioners shared their observations to make this list. They were in no doubt that the most likely victims were:

- Fragile children, for example small, slightly built children who do not meet the criterion of 'being big'. They can be targeted because they appear unlikely to retaliate.
- Vulnerable children who appear distressed or reluctant to join in, fearing they will be hurt or unable to cope.
- Children who cannot follow the unwritten rules of someone else's game, so they get left out. They are not allowed to play, and that hurts.
- Those who are different in any way that makes them stand out from the rest, such as grubby or overweight children.

- Children who have a learning difference or disability, such as dyspraxia, attention deficit hyperactivity disorder (ADHD), Asperger's syndrome or Tourette's syndrome, because their difficulties may not be understood and other children do not understand why they bump all the time or make loud noises or do not respond to their overtures in the usual way. Interestingly, it is often the case that children with obvious differences, such as those with Down's syndrome, may be nurtured or even swamped by benign attentions, showing that compassion can be intuitive or be aroused in most children. Sadly, however, hurtful name calling can affect these children too.
- The most able children who know all the answers and converse in more adult ways. They can be resented if they are given different curriculum materials or more challenging activities, or take up too much of the teacher's time. And they may be isolated or called geeks because they use difficult or technical vocabulary that the others do not understand.
- Those who find it difficult to cope, perhaps because they have poor memories and need constant reminders so that instructions interrupt the flow of teaching; those who fluff even simple tasks; the ones who cannot cope with changes in routine; the ones who cannot find their own belongings and perhaps inadvertently take someone else's; those who vent their frustration on others.
- Children who have habits that offend the rest.

But there are always exceptions. Listen to David explaining his predicament:

> My lad, Gordon, is a big chap; he's very gentle and used to looking out for his brother so I didn't anticipate any problems at nursery. At first he was happy but after a week or two he didn't want to go and when I asked him why, he said that a boy was hitting him.
>
> I said, 'Watch out for him and just don't go near him', but this other child sought Gordon out. After a bit when things didn't improve, I decided to go to the staff and explain. The practitioners were amazed. 'Who is it?' they asked and I nearly died when the 'culprit' appeared! He was up to Gordon's elbow, a tiny child. Gordon could have sorted him out, no bother. The staff had no suspicion that my apparently happy-go-lucky child was so upset but they took time to explain: 'Always come to us – you are a good boy for not hitting him back.' In private, one member of staff confided that 'the wee nippy ones are often the worst'.

So, nothing can be taken for granted. Looking big and strong does not automatically exempt children from being bullied!

Question 8: Does making children aware of the effects of bullying make them stop?

The hope was that the answer to this question would be an unequivocal 'yes', but some children have not developed the altruism or empathy to allow them to understand someone else's perspective or the effects of their actions. Or they have other reasons for continuing, such as the fact that it is the quickest and surest way to get what they want.

Grace, an experienced primary school headteacher, explains:

> I hope that bullying is less prevalent than it was, but, sadly, I suspect – in fact, I know – that there are still bullies in every class. The staff:student ratio is higher in the nursery than in Key Stages 1 and 2 and there are more harder-to-supervise moments as the children grow, even if it's just moving from one classroom to another or going down to the hall. And some children start bullying when they go outside and are wide-eyed and innocent when they are tackled after break. We allow upset children to stay in the hall now and a playground supervisor stays with them. As we want them to have fresh air, it's not the best solution, but better than them being distressed. But of course these arrangements can lead to bullying too when children are told they are scaredy-cats, too frightened to come out to play.

Indoors, of course, has its own set of issues. Grace continued:

> The children are much more aware of opportunities for causing annoyance as they grow and sometimes I think they try things out to see how far they can go. Some of them know that staff have few sanctions and a telling-off doesn't worry them – in fact, they consider it a bonus. So, children who happen to be in the way get bumped aside as rough children surge past in the narrow corridors. It's always the same children and sometimes staff can consider that the hurt ones overreact by crying or making a huge fuss, but of course that doesn't excuse aggressive behaviour or make the pain any less.
>
> The differences between the children's academic abilities are much more obvious to them in primary school (Key Stages 2 and

3), for at this time they can be striving to meet targets. We have groups for different topics and try to mix the children socially when we can, but they know the children in the top groups. It doesn't matter how we disguise the names. It can be very hard for some children and some parents to accept that other children find learning easier, and when this hits home, they react in negative, self-defeating ways. I remember reading an article called 'Having a laugh'. It was by David Wood, if I remember, and it explained that underachievers often acted in a 'don't care' way so that when they didn't make the grade they could explain that they weren't trying anyway. I'm sure even some of our young children do that.

Asked how she tackled this issue, Grace explained:

Well, we try to stress that being caring and kind is very important, and they all are capable of that, but of course you don't get a mark or a grade for looking out for others, so the children see it as being of lesser importance – as do their parents! Somehow we've got our educational priorities all wrong.

(See Chapter 6 for strategies and ideas to stop bullying.)

Next Grace was asked about gifted and talented children. Did the new emphasis on recognising and reporting their abilities make them more prone to bullying? She replied:

'Again it depends on the child. Some are very confident, delighted to be ahead, and if they are teased, they can shrug it off because they have the skills and abilities that are important to them. They don't appear to care or even notice if they are left out of games because they don't want to play these games anyway. They would rather research a favourite topic than play football. I heard one child call to a bright one, 'When I'm grown up I'll be richer than you because you can't play football.' The reply was 'But I'll be on the continent of Africa helping poor children. That's miles better than kicking a ball!'

But of course other gifted and talented children pine to be one of the crowd, and bullies can hurt them by name calling just the same as the others. Sometimes in class these children will get things wrong just to prove they are the same as their peers. Suddenly they can stop answering or volunteering to take responsibility. They refute the idea that they have talents and gifts because these make them different. It's a real challenge to get teaching at the right level without isolating them. We can't allow them to underachieve.

Question 9: What are the most common forms of bullying that you see happening?

Leah, a Foundation-stage teacher, commented:

In the upper primary especially, bullying behaviour becomes more difficult to spot. It's not the quick punch or the name calling any more; rather, it's covert incidents that are harder to prove. Hiding someone's things or spoiling them . . . threatening that something will happen later . . . telling someone they'll be left out . . . laughing at someone's clothes or shoes – all devastating, and not done where a member of staff can see.

Then there's the parents. They can be bullies too. You'd think they would want to work with the school, and of course many do – but you'd be surprised! Very often the parents stress the children out. I find that the children who bully are often afraid of letting their parents down. Parents' expectations can be completely unrealistic, given the child's abilities, and even in the light of their own achievements. Some blame their children for lack of success and others blame the school. When staff were told that all reports sent home had to have only positive comments, many parents were given unrealistic ideas of what their children could achieve, and when work became more formal and progress slowed down, staff were blamed. This all adds to the pressure for us as well as the children.

Leah continued:

In addition to all of this, some children see bullying as fun. When I asked Tom why he was horrid to Andrew, he told me it was because 'he'll cry in a minute – he's a baby, that's why'. Tom showed no sign of being sorry at all; in fact, he enjoyed taunting the other children, even if it landed him in trouble. That's how bitter some 6-year-olds can be.

She explained further:

Another difficulty is that when one kind of behaviour is named as bullying and therefore unacceptable, the perpetrators can find another to put in its place. And often the upset victim can often find it impossible to explain what has gone on because they've been told not to tell tales, which means that steps to sort the problem can be delayed. When I said to Josie, 'I'm watching you and no hitting will be allowed', she sloped off, but later I caught her nipping the same child. 'I didn't hit,' she shouted, 'so you can't blame me!' We have had to assign a member of staff to watch her specifically because a few of the more timid children were waiting for her to strike. From one day to the next they never knew what to expect, and that was affecting their confidence. One or two children were becoming more and more clingy and miserable, not wanting to go outside to play, and that's just not acceptable.

Josie's parents didn't want to know. Leah continued, ' "She's not aggressive at home," they claimed, implying that it was our fault or that we were making it up, and that was that!' And as the children can key in to their parents' attitude, problems persist.

Question 10: Does the type of bullying change?

Grace raised the issue of the type of bullying changing as the children grew. One study that investigated the type of bullying and separated the results by gender was carried out by Bee (1999). This showed the percentage of boys and girls aged 4–11 rated by their teachers as displaying each type of behaviour.

Type of behaviour	Boys	Girls
Mean to others	21.8	9.6
Physical attacks	18.1	4.4
Gets involved in many fights	30.9	9.8
Destroys others' things	10.6	4.4
Destroys self/own possessions	10.7	2.1

The gender difference, she explained is apparent even at 4 years old. Girls are much more likely to use relational aggression (e.g. 'I'll get my Daddy to you – he's a policeman') or bribery (e.g. 'I won't ask you to my party unless . . .'). Or they make sly faces. It is also revealing to note that girls tend to bully other girls! They are also more likely to run to an adult to complain. Boys, on the other hand, tend to use physical aggression but get less emotionally involved, at least on the surface. They see bullying as par for the course, something that has to be expected and endured. They either hit back or crumple but tend not to 'tell' until things have escalated – and of course the difficulties for both bully and victim are then more entrenched.

These differences show that there are different types of bullying behaviours depending on the innate characteristics of the children, including their gender and temperament as well as the environmental and cultural experiences they have had. The difference also depends on each child's level of empathy and altruism, key developments in recognising how others feel.

So, the type of behaviour used does change over time – from the overt physical abuse in the early years to the covert, sly innuendoes later on. Bee (1999) explains the shift from what she calls 'instrumental aggression' to 'hostile aggression'. An example of instrumental aggression could be a 3-year-old knocking over another child in order to grab a toy or sit at the front of the group. The hurt child was in the wrong place at the wrong time rather than being targeted as a victim, as is the case when aggression becomes hostile. Frustration plays a big part here. Early years children are often frustrated by not being allowed to do what they wish, and because they cannot express these wishes coherently, they express their frustration through aggression. But most often as the children develop language skills and become able to carry out more independent tasks, their level of physical aggression drops.

Hostile aggression is different in that it consists of premeditated and repeated acts carried out in the knowledge that the recipients will be caused anguish or physical hurt. Primary-age children with more developed language skills can use inflection and non-verbal communication, or even sarcasm and innuendoes, to hurt the feelings of others. The hurt can arise from the way things are said rather than the words themselves. The variety of bullying behaviour increases, yet incidents can be difficult to spell out and can sound petty in the retelling. This is one reason why children find it so hard to explain, and it prevents them sharing their fears.

Texting and emailing

Unfortunately, technological advances have opened up another avenue for bullying. Colin, a school manager, explains:

> We had a spell of children bringing phones into school and soon they became a status symbol, and then there were incidents when they were stolen or damaged or lost. Then some children began texting nasty messages, so we don't allow mobile phones in school now. The children have to hand them to the teachers at the start of the day and they are locked away. If a problem does occur coming to school or on the way home, we tell the children that all texts can be traced. But it's really down to the parents. Staff can't take responsibility for the children's actions once they are out of school. Some parents complain about children being upset by blogs on the Internet at home. The school needs a clear policy explaining that to parents. They have to deal with that sort of thing. It's not in our remit.

Question 11: Is bullying a common problem or do one or two events get built up out of proportion? How many children say they were bullied or admit to being bullies?

To answer the question of how common bullying is, we have to look at statistics for primary-age children (Todd *et al.* 2004). We also have to remember that admitting being bullied – even anonymously – is hard and that these figures may only show the tip of the iceberg.

The main findings of the report by Todd *et al.* (2004) are as follows:

- Around 1 in 12 pupils say they have been bullied and around 1 in 20 say they have bullied others at a frequency of at least four times in the past two months.
- A higher percentage of boys than girls report that they have bullied others while reports of being bullied are the same for both genders.
- Reports of being bullied declined between 1994 and 2002.
- Fighting is more commonly reported by boys than by girls.
- Around 1 in 7 pupils say they have been in a fight three times or more in the last year.

Interestingly, the researchers (ibid.) found that in Scotland more children fought than were verbally bullied, while in England verbal bullying was more prevalent than fighting! In the cross-country table derived from measuring the prevalence of bullying, English scores were higher than the Scottish ones and the Welsh were just between the two. The Irish results showed the lowest scores in the British Isles (Todd *et al.* 2004).

Question 12: Is bullying something that only belongs to childhood?

Apparently bullying occurs in adult life too; many adults are still bullies or victims. Murray and Keane (1998) have revealed some frightening statistics. They claim that

- 20 per cent of children are afraid to go to school:
- 38 per cent of primary-age children report they have been distressed to the extent that their lifestyle has been harmed;
- 15 per cent of women are affected by sexual bullying;
- 15 per cent of men are bullied at work;
- 25 per cent of adults, even old people, suffer physical and/or verbal abuse;
- 14 per cent of suicides are associated with bullying.

It can be seen, then, that bullying causes enormous hurt and damage that can last for a lifetime, or even cause a life to be extinguished. It is the continual nastiness, real or even imagined, that can sap confidence and competence. The anticipation – that is, not knowing what will happen or where it will occur – can be as overwhelming as the incidents themselves.

Question 13: Are all bullies the same?

It is important to distinguish between the different types because therein lies a clue to giving the most appropriate kind of support.

Reactive bullies

Reactive bullies are children who have experienced significant hurt or been overwhelmed by events either inside nursery or school, or at home. Divorce, bereavement, even a best friend moving away – the children lash out in frustration at their inability to remedy the situation. Their wish is to recapture life as it was. They have to be comforted and reassured that 'it's OK to be sad' (Collins 2005) and that happy times will come soon.

Anxious bullies

Anxious bullies are the children who show deep-seated insecurity and they attempt to gain status through bullying. Their self-esteem is low. The bullying may be a self-preservation mechanism, but other children can recognise what is going on and encourage the child to continue the unacceptable behaviour, perhaps to deflect attention from themselves. The anxious child may actually be cast in a role he or she does not want, but cannot work out how to change it.

Underachieving bullies

Underachieving bullies are children who compensate for their lack of progress in academic subjects by bullying others. Often they adopt a 'don't care' attitude or insist they are 'having a laugh', but deep down they may be despairing.

One strategy here is to give equal time and accord to different curriculum areas and give deserved public praise when the children do something worthwhile such as helping to gather in books or footballs, or taking the lunch money to the office. Thus, the child is given responsibility for worthwhile tasks. This strategy may well be rejected at first because responsibility can be demanding and lead to failure, but carefully chosen tasks can lead to a real feeling of accomplishment and trust.

Home experience bullies

Many bullies come from problem backgrounds where bullying behaviour between adults and children and between children is the norm. These children are beset by a myriad of problems such as poverty, abuse, drugs – all kinds of living on the edge. Some parents or carers may use harsh discipline, including physical punishment, to enforce rules. This punishment can be unexpected and given for no obvious (to the child) misdemeanour. Family problems sometimes cause members to lash out. The children may come to believe that such punishment is deserved, so they grow up afraid or rebellious or accepting. With the only role model one of physical retaliation, the children in turn hit out without considering the consequences whenever they are thwarted or displeased.

It is understandable that they cannot rationalise their actions because they have lived in this regime. They have no other experience to draw upon. Practitioners are wary of criticising the parents, and this makes explanations to the children difficult. Saying, 'in this class, we do it this way . . .' seems the best immediate strategy, although examples and discussions have to be made explicit.

All of these types of bullies need support and positive feedback. These children are usually willing to listen, evaluate and agree to change their actions if these are explained in a non-judgemental way. Their actions can be a cry for help.

Sadistic bullies

And there are the dyed-in-the-wool bullies who show no regard for others' feelings. They mock any attempt to reason. They defy parents and teachers. They seem to enjoy inflicting pain. They have no altruism or empathy. They become the 'hard nut' bullies and may eventually find that only other children of like mind will tolerate them as 'friends'. In this way gangs are formed. Bullies of this kind do not appear to care for their own well-being or that of others. They may have a conduct disorder such as oppositional behaviour disorder (OBD) or another neurobiological disorder requiring medical attention.

> We have children that stare you out, who know they are untouchable no matter what they do. And of course their parents are right behind them. Exclusion isn't the answer because these children would rather be at home watching television anyway. You just need one like this and the whole atmosphere is spoiled.
>
> (Teacher, Year 4 class)

It can be hard for these children to accept that they do need help to adopt different ways of behaving, and they will usually robustly deny that change is required. This causes resentment, and many parents and teachers, after they have tried all the positive approaches and the 'catch them being good' techniques, want bullies to be excluded from school. This is because they disrupt learning for all the other children and may cause them physical as well as emotional harm.

Question 14: What do children say about the different ways children bully?

Seven-year-old Jake explains:

> The worst thing about bullying is waiting for it to happen. I know that calling me names doesn't hurt like getting hit but it's awful not knowing when it's going to happen or if they'll do it again. And the worst thing is that when they start, people I've been playing with go away. They don't want the bullies to do it to them, so I'm left on my own and I feel there's nothing I can do. If I tell, then they'll get me on the way home and my Dad can't pick me up because he's working. I used to be happy at this school and I don't know why everything has changed but I can't stand much more. I'm going to move to a different school, my Dad says.

Eight-year-old Aaron tells his sad tale:

> I asked my Mum why she had called me Aaron. In the playground they were shouting, 'Aaron, keep your hair on', or worse, 'Aaron's got no hair on.' Then they were calling Robbie 'Robbie the jobbie', so we got together and decided we'd pretend to laugh at them. It was easier when there were two of us. My Mum said to ignore them and they'd get bored, but how long do we have to wait? The teacher said to shout out 'sticks and stones will break my bones but names will never hurt me', but that doesn't stop them either.

Ten-year-old Gail found that

> It's better if you get hit because then you get to go into school and you aren't called names for ratting. And sometimes the person that helps you will stay and chat for a bit. If you are just called names, no one cares.

These three young people have identified the loneliness of the victim as being very hard to deal with. One of the strategies often suggested to victims is 'stay in a crowd because bullies tend to pick on children who are on their own'. Did this work for Jess? No! 'I try to stay near the others,' she explained, 'but they go off in their groups and turn their backs on me. Why does no one want to help?'

There are so many behaviours that isolate and demean children.

Question 15: Does the way the victim reacts sustain the bully?

No child should have to adopt a coping mechanism just to reduce the chance of being bullied. 'Every child should be able to be themselves' (Todd *et al.* 2004). However, Byrne (2003) insists that 'The reaction to negative behaviour is crucial in determining whether that behaviour will be repeated'. He claims that 'While almost everyone will be tested, not everyone will be bullied' (ibid.), suggesting that monitoring the child's reaction to events offers a clue to intervention. At the common sense level, parents and professionals often wish the child being bullied would 'stand up for themselves or laugh – somehow they have to show they don't care'. While this is very difficult, it can empower the victim (see Chapter 6 for strategies and ideas).

The only safe solution is for the school to explain to children who bully is that if they don't change their behaviour, in a very short time no one will like them. And if this first communication does not work, then sanctions, even exclusion, will be put in place. Guidance provided in Ireland (Department of Education 1993) where the incidence of bullying was lower than in the United Kingdom, states explicitly that:

- If you are involved, you will be warned to stop. A second occurrence means that a record will be made in the incident book.
- If you continue, your parents will be informed and privileges will be removed
- If the incident is serious, you will be suspended.

The staff claim that making children aware that all instances of unacceptable behaviour will be recorded is a powerful deterrent.

Question 16: How can staff protect their children from being bullied?

The key action is to offer reassurance, so helping the children to feel safe. Strategies that have been found helpful are given by a group of primary staff who formed an anti-bullying group. They chose their most successful six hints.

- If the victim has disclosed the problem, praise their courage in doing so.
- Reassure the victim that the problem lies with the bullies and that he or she is not to blame.

- Tell the victim that you recognise his or her anxiety and its cause and that you are taking steps to stop the bullying happening again
- Arrange to meet the child the following week so that he or she knows that the concern has not been brushed aside and that the bully is being observed.
- Ascertain who in the child's class is likely to bully, for more than one may bully the same child, and establish basic safeguards such as 'Stay near the playground supervisor' or 'Stay indoors at playtime for a bit'.
- Ask the child about any strategies he or she may have considered, such as smiling, offering to forgive the bully or being strong, saying things such as 'I'm not wanting a friend like you.'

On a personal one-to-one level, the group decided to ask children who were victims:

- Who is the friendliest child in your class?
- Who would stand up for you if the teacher gave him that special job?
- Do you think the bully realises how you feel? Should we explain that you are unhappy?
- Does the bully live near you at home?
- What can we do to make you feel safe again?

The children were also encouraged to do some assertiveness training (see Chapter 5).

Question 17: But what about the bullies? Do we need to listen to them?

Certainly the bullies must have a fair chance to explain their understanding of events, for a number of reasons:

- No one may have explained what a bully is, and the children who are blamed may not have worked this out for themselves.
- An unintentional hurt may have been blown up out of proportion.
- The victim may make too much of the episode. (This is why the recording of bullying behaviour often emphasises the descriptor 'repetitive'.)
- The bullies may be brash and aggressive to hide feelings of inadequacy and low self-esteem.

It is vital that confronting the bullies is done calmly, if possible conveying respect for the children while decrying their behaviour. Any other scenario could make the outcome worse for the victim because there are many out-of-the-way corners bullies might choose.

Note that bullies and victims should not be asked to explain their disagreements or grievances together unless the victim has assured staff that this is acceptable. If they choose to do this, using Edward de Bono's 'six thinking hats' strategy is a helpful way to diffuse the situation (see the Appendix).

Question 18: Do children always 'tell?'

Unfortunately, there is the unwritten but enduring cultural rule that 'telling tales' is beyond the pale. Children have to understand the difference between that and acting responsibly, and they have to be assured of support when they do. Practitioners, either overtly through explanations or more covertly by providing opportunities for a private moment with individual children in turn, have to create an atmosphere where it is safe to speak out.

Often children on the autistic spectrum do not tell because they do not realise that their parents and teachers do not already know. This is very sad for them as they are denied protection, and hugely perplexing for their parents, left as they often are in the dark. It is some solace for them to recognise, however, that one aspect of their child's condition – that is, not being able to interpret the non-verbal communication of others – may protect their children from recognising the sneers and sidelong glances that are often so hurtful.

Many other victims do not tell because they feel that they are to blame.

> I wish I could shout out 'get lost' but I just can't. One teacher made me stand in front of a mirror to practise saying, 'I don't want a friend like you,' but when I tried that, this horrid boy yelled out 'Some chance you've got' and the others laughed. I try not to be a victim but land up getting hurt anyway. It's not fair because I don't do bad things but I don't get friends either.

Sometimes victims who have tried to tell feel that their worries have been brushed aside. Rob explains:

> My Dad told me that bullying is just part of school life and the sooner I learn to cope the easier it will be. He said, 'Shoulders

back – show them what you are made of – tell them you are not putting up with any of their rubbish', and it worked. In fact, one or two boys told me we would make a new group because they didn't want to be bullied either. So I felt like a leader instead.

Question 19: Do staff ever bully?

In the eyes of the children and even colleagues, some practitioners certainly do! Helen, aged 6, tells her story:

> I'm trying my best but I know that other people will have much better drawings than me and be better at everything else as well. When the teacher comes round I know she's going to shout out my name. 'Come on, Helen. You can do better than that,' she'll say, and the others snigger. My tummy goes into knots and I have to squeeze my eyes to stop crying. Sometimes she says, 'I've told you that already', and I know she has, but I can't remember what it was. So I can't do it and then I get into trouble again.
>
> When I get things wrong at home, my mum says, 'God Almighty . . .' but I know teachers aren't allowed to say that. But that's what they are thinking, so I just try to get through the day and I play in the park on my way home. I wish I had a friend to come with me.

Helen is highlighting the loneliness that often accompanies being a victim. No wonder some despair.

Discussing this, practitioners made a list of things from their past and current experience that could be construed as bullying:

- Calling out a child's name too often.
- Giving too little attention to a child.
- Giving too many instructions, for example 'Do this and then that' when some children who have planning and sequencing difficulties find this impossible.
- Not accommodating learning differences in terms of pacing or differentiation.
- Insisting on changing an activity when the children are engrossed in what they are doing.
- Making children clear away someone else's resources or mess.
- Saying one child's work is good and not commenting on another's.
- Looking out over the classroom when listening to a child so that the child realises that the practitioner is distracted.

- Not giving each child responsible jobs, but involving only a few.
- Being brusque when a child is in distress, for example 'Oh no, not again, you must really learn to . . .'
- Not smiling enough to encourage the children to relax.
- Changing the anticipated routine of the day (which can upset many children).
- Giving too much homework so that some less intellectually able children spend the whole day and most of the evening failing to cope. They get no release from feeling a failure and resentment builds up.

Such possibilities make everyone stop and think!

Question 20: Do teachers always know?

Unless children are up front – and this can be extremely difficult when feelings of guilt or failure are combining with many children's natural reluctance to make a fuss or stand out from the group – even the most caring teachers may genuinely not know.

Many children learn to disguise their emotions so that facial expressions and even body language (that is, non-verbal communications) do not give clues as to how they really feel. So, victims explain their tears as 'having a sore tummy' while children who have bullied can appear guilt-free. Sometimes children will restrain any outward signs of unhappiness all day and explode when they go home. Or signs may be subtle, and in a busy class of over twenty young people, the demands of just getting through the curriculum may prevent bullying being recognised.

And of course the staff in turn may not realise how they appear to their children. Many adults reflecting on their schooldays remember first the teacher who caused them anguish, even prevented them taking risks because getting something wrong merited retribution. How complex it all is!

2 Prime targets
Children with learning differences

I wanted to come to school today
I thought things would be better
The teacher said that she would act
My mum had sent a letter.

But when these big boys crowded in
I began to shake all over,
There was no-one to make them go,
I had to run for cover.

I don't know why they bully me
I can't help that I'm lame,
No-one wants to play with me.
I always get the blame.

Joseph, aged 9

Sometimes bullying is not only what people do, it's what they don't do to help you.

The policy of inclusion means that many more children with a range of more complex needs are being educated in mainstream classrooms. With sound support and resource provision, some can thrive on the opportunities and social interactions mainstream provides, but for others 'the busy, buzzing classroom may alienate and confuse' (Moore 2004). The setting itself can increase vulnerability through giving sensory overload and making children less able to cope. So, the policy of inclusion can also mean that some children with learning differences are prone to be bullied, especially if the other children do not understand what their difficulties are or if they or their parents resent any extra attention or resource provision these children require.

Some children with some conditions appear to settle in mainstream settings more readily than others. Many children with Down's syndrome, as one example, have better social skills than those on the autistic spectrum, and these help them cope. Some of these children may have limited speech but their understanding is good and often they are smiling, engaging and responsive, especially in the early years. This helps them make friends. And as a result of interacting with articulate peers, their language skills improve, and many are surpassing earlier expectations, given their lower IQ status (Buckley 2007). Although these children do best with a visual curriculum, which requires teachers to make special resources, other visual learners benefit too, and this sharing can foster interactions and shared learning. Moreover, the fact that other children recognise the features of Down's syndrome helps nurture empathy and altruism in others, especially if the children chosen or volunteering to be 'buddies' are overtly praised for the support they give. But perhaps the fact that, although there can be tantrums at 4 years (these are more usually associated with the 2-year-old stage, but delayed because of the later development in children with Down's syndrome), there are no sustained and disruptive behavioural difficulties associated with the condition eases their acceptance with teachers and other parents. So, these children are less likely to be bullied than others with special needs conditions; in fact, they may be swamped by children wanting to look after them and do for them things they could perfectly well do for themselves. As they grow, however, more children with Down's syndrome will be bullied, especially by other children who do not understand what is wrong, or by those who are reacting against being taunted themselves, or by sadistic bullies looking for 'easy' victims.

Asked about bullying incidents concerning a whole range of children with additional support needs, headteacher Pamela replied:

> It is so sad that children who already have an extra struggle to cope with the activities of daily living and/or the content of the curriculum are the very ones who very often are targeted by bullies. I doubt if there is a school that would claim that this doesn't happen. Many of our children with additional needs can be baffled by not understanding either the cause or the intention of taunts and so they don't understand how to respond. They may not understand the language or even the meaning of what is said, so they appear ready to cry and this can encourage the bullies to carry on. Even worse, these children may not be able to visualise the implications of carrying out a bully's instructions.

In their wish to have a friend, they do as they are told. This can mean taking risks, with sometimes dangerous results. At the very least, the potential friendship, i.e. the 'reward', doesn't materialise, and that can devastate hopes and dreams; in the worst-case scenario the children can be both physically and mentally scarred. We try to ensure that each child has a buddy, but with the greater number of children with a whole variety of needs coming into every school, it can be hard to find youngsters who would rather befriend a less able child than play football. And, of course, statistically and realistically there are many more boys than girls, and boys can resent having a girl for a buddy. Sometimes a boy will give up his football to take his turn at befriending and then the child with additional needs is off sick and he feels he has lost out on both counts. And of course providing a buddy can be a way of labelling children. You need the wisdom of Job to get it right!

Pamela raised the issue of children with difficulties being off sick. Are they less robust than other children? Could this possibly be related to bullying?

Carter (2000) explains that even anticipating being bullied is a huge stress, and when this is unremitting day after day, the stress hormones are activated. These should be supporting the immune system, but when they are asked to do a different job, the immune system is less well protected and the children can be left prone to illnesses and infections and so miss school. Missing school can offer a temporary relief from being bullied, but the children's education suffers and another potential source of bullying – lagging behind – comes into play.

An extremely worrying aftermath of severe bullying is that the victim can be left with what appears to the onlooker to be irrational phobias (Carter 2000). If victims are traumatised, they may not be able to recall the face of the bully or begin to describe the incident. Later, however, even when safely away from the source of stress, they can develop phobias about red hair or blue eyes, or whatever the characteristics of the bully are. This can be inexplicable to carers and debilitating to the victim long after the bullying incident has occurred. Parents and school professionals may not realise that the stress hormones energised by the incident have caused the difficulty. This can let bullies off the hook, too, because suspicions are not enough. Real evidence is needed to justify intervention.

Autistic spectrum disorders

Listen to some parents now. First, hear Charlotte Moore, mother of George and Sam, two very different boys who both have autism (she is also author of the wonderful book *George and Sam* (Moore 2004)). From her own experiences and her communications with other parents of children with additional support needs, she is certain that children who are different 'will be bullied – it's par for the course. And they don't tell because they think you already know.' As both George and Sam had difficulties in reading the non-verbal communication of their peers, these difficulties being symptoms of autism, they found responding appropriately in different and changing contexts confusing, and this difference led to their being picked on. Why didn't they explain their plight or ask for help? Charlotte Moore reveals that her children 'thought she already knew'. They didn't appreciate that she couldn't know about events when she was not present. This raises a whole new issue for practitioners caring for children on the autistic spectrum. If these children do not or cannot explain what is going on, then observations professionals make have to be continuous and that bit more perceptive. Perhaps practitioners have to make their lack of understanding of events explicit by saying to the children, 'I was not there, and I do not know what happened. Please tell me everything you can.' At the same time they have to recognise that the bullied children's recall may be 'paralysed' by their stress hormones and so this might be an inappropriate request. Perhaps the buddies have to share this understanding and develop sensitive eyes and ears.

Another part of autism and Asperger's syndrome (often called high-functioning autism, meaning that the children have a higher level of intelligence than others labelled autistic, but they have the same difficulties with communication) is that children do not understand colloquialisms. They take language literally. One child with autism was cruelly asked, 'Have you lost your marbles?' His reply about never having had marbles was met by loud jeers and further taunts. He was left bewildered and hurt.

Children on the spectrum may not respond to requests to 'come and play', or they may attempt to join in but be baffled by trying to follow the unwritten rules of someone else's game. Children constantly change their role play and expect others to adapt seamlessly to the change. Most of the meaning and sequence of this change is contained in the facial expressions or body language, rather than in any verbal explanation of what is going on, so children on the autistic spectrum who cannot interpret these non-verbal communications are lost. When they make inappropriate responses, the bullies pounce.

It is fascinating and salutary to realise that children who are on the spectrum very rarely bully. Perhaps this is because they are not sufficiently interested in and so do not covet what other children have. They are rarely self-proud or selfish. One child, asked why he gave his toy away, immediately answered, 'because he [Peter] wanted it'. This is a typical, obvious – to them – kind of answer! How can one explain to a child who cannot foresee the implications of his actions that other children might take advantage of his generosity?

Another facet of the disability is obsessive interests, for example in collecting items. These can be overpowering for children on the spectrum yet be mystifying to neurotypical children. 'Why does Grant snatch my sweets then tear the paper off and give me the sweet back?', asked baffled Dane. The answer was of course that only the paper interested Grant, and to him it was crucially important as he had a collection of sweet wrappers that gave him tremendous satisfaction. Unfortunately, children can shy away from activities that to them are senseless and strange, and if they share their observations with others, then the disquiet grows.

Many teachers explain that their greatest concern is the greater number of children presenting with autistic spectrum-type difficulties. In one town alone, 'the number of recorded diagnoses doubled over a four year period' (Keen and Ward 2004). This appeared to be due to a greater recognition of ASD in more able children and in those with ADHD as well as parents being more aware of the early signs. The greater incidence means that understanding the children's experiences in being bullied is vitally important.

Speech and language difficulties

Sometimes parents, teachers and other onlookers can confuse speech and language impairments with autistic spectrum disorders. This is because 'the boundaries between classic autism and other disorders are not clearly defined' (Barrett *et al.* 2004). Children who have social interaction and communication difficulties, who cannot speak clearly, who stutter or who cannot enact the 'rules' of conversation (timing, turn taking, the use of phatics) are other candidates for being bullied. Many children who have learning differences but who are not autistic share language impairments such as echolalia, odd intonation, and/or severe difficulties in the pragmatic or conversational aspects of language. (This has recently been renamed pragmatic impairment (PI).) Children with these difficulties show high levels of withdrawal and poor motivation, and are less accepted by their peer group. Some may have poor impulse control and, without an accurate label, be viewed as having attention deficit disorder (ADD) or ADHD. Rejection leads to isolation and possible victimisation, and if the children are less responsive to adult solicitations, then providing a stimulating curriculum is challenging indeed. The children's plight is unimaginable if they are bullied yet cannot explain what went on.

Dyspraxia, or developmental coordination disorder

Life can be equally demeaning for highly articulate, intelligent children with learning differences such as dyspraxia (*dys* = faulty, *praxis* = the ability to use the body as a skilled tool), or developmental coordination disorder (DCD). Listen to part of an interview with 10-year-old Aaron talking with Dr Amanda Kirby at her Dyscovery Centre, a private clinic for supporting children with learning differences. Aaron's parents were mystified that their bright son couldn't do things every other child could do. His mother explained:

> Buttons were horrendous and he spent so long trying to get ready for school and got so upset that I had to do things for him. Yet he was as bright as anything. I began to think there was something wrong with me as a teacher . . . there must be a knack to tying laces that I didn't know.

When Dr Kirby asked Aaron about his writing (often a key worry for children and their parents), he replied:

> It's worse than anyone else in the whole class. I can see in my head how I want to do it and I try to do it that way, but when it goes down to my hand it goes all wrong somehow.

He did lack finger and arm strength and he had some timing problems evident in his lack of skill in catching a ball and using a knife and fork as well as being last to get dressed after PE lessons. These coordination difficulties had caused the whole family great distress because they did not understand what was wrong, and, of course, despite assurances to the contrary, Aaron felt he had let his parents down.

How did the other children react? Was he bullied? Aaron was able to explain his experiences and left us in no doubt that this was the case:

They told me I was dumb, I was crazy; I was a bit funny up here [pointing to his temple]. And when Dr Kirby asked, 'Did you think you were?' Aaron replied, 'Well, after a while I began to believe them. One girl actually told me I was handicapped, that I shouldn't be at this school.

Fortunately, the Centre was able to provide a programme to help Aaron's motor control, and gradually, as his competence increased, his confidence was re-established too, but how many other children out there are suffering similar fates? When they have movement difficulties they are public; the other children can see what is amiss and, taunting, cause them to lose belief in their own global abilities. They transfer feelings of inadequacy in one area to the others where they may well be perfectly competent. Perhaps this is the source of Neihart's (2003) advice. She explains:

> When you have a child with a particular difficulty, focus on the things he does well and at the same time pay attention to the things that are difficult. If you only concentrate on the difficulties, then the child's self-esteem will suffer.

How often do anxious teachers and parents concentrate on trying to make up ground on the things that are problematic? They may not realise that if children are faced with constant catch-up activities, their sense of failure becomes entrenched.

This raises the issue of homework. If children have spent the day feeling they are failures, surely their evenings must engender success? Children with dyspraxia and other difficulties often have exercise programmes to practise in the evenings, and 'getting homework done' can tip the family over the edge.

Listen now to Sally, who is Jason and Gillian's mother. Both her children have additional support needs.

> I try to be calm, for Jason's so tired all of the time. This is because he has to concentrate so hard to carry out instructions. Someone at the clinic explained that this was due to poor habituation. This means that instead of tasks becoming automatic, he has to begin each one from scratch. This all needs extra concentration and causes great stress. So, he falls behind and if he comes home with stuff he didn't finish in class, he just refuses to do it and we end up screaming at one another. Homework is the straw that breaks my back.

Who are the bullies now? Well-meaning professionals have to remember that parents have challenges too and try to ease their interactions with their child, not make them worse.

The attention deficit disorders

Attention deficit disorder

Sally was distressed to find that her daughter Gillian had elements of attention deficit disorder (ADD) co-occurring with her earlier diagnosis of dyspraxia. She explained that Gillian needed to make a specific effort to concentrate and remember things, for

> she forgets all of the time. Even when I write notes she forgets to read them and she's not being naughty. She gets really upset by forgetting. She forgets things she wants to do, not just things she would rather avoid.

Gillian's teacher explained that in class

> she spends a great deal of time daydreaming – she doesn't focus for long and then she just switches off. So, she doesn't achieve much. I don't want her to work with the children who are not so bright but as she rarely gets anything finished, what am I to do? Then the other children ask what group she's in and she gets upset. She knows she's capable of so much more but I've got to have evidence rather than just a gut feeling. I tried putting the large egg timer on her desk and asked her to concentrate as hard as she can till the sand runs through but she appeared mesmerised watching the sand and of course the other children wanted to know why the timer was there in the first place. I soon realised that making her feel different wasn't kind, especially as she gets distressed by falling behind. It's hard to know what to try. She doesn't cause any fuss, she just dreams the time away.

Being able to pay attention and remember is a competence that comes naturally to most children even though they may decide not to exercise it. This genuine lack of ability to pay attention can cause much unhappiness, for the result – children asking for instructions to be repeated or withdrawing from learning so that they must be – can be misdiagnosed as laziness. Many children affected by ADD find they cannot cut out distracters in the environment. Things like flickering lights or buzzing noises or simply the general rustle of a busy classroom defeat their efforts to ignore them. Girls tend to have this form of the condition more than boys, and they tend to withdraw from learning by daydreaming. Naturally, not paying attention prevents them from realising their potential, yet they can be very intelligent children. Parents, teachers and the children themselves can become very frustrated!

Attention deficit hyperactivity disorder

But why should some children not be able to pay attention? And why is paying attention so important? Most of us have been brought up being told to 'pay attention' in class, and although we didn't always obey, we had no doubt that if we were that way inclined, we could attend and learn. Unfortunately, some children just cannot. And when poor attention is combined with hyperactivity (ADHD) – and this affects more boys than girls – the child's inability to be quiet and still can disrupt lessons and annoy everyone in the class, which can easily lead to bullying. Other parents, even those who understand the condition, can become less than sympathetic when they fear their own children's learning will suffer. Yet these children simply cannot control their urge to move. Something out there is usually more interesting than the task at hand, and yet when the children's interests are really aroused, they can concentrate and be still and produce work of high quality.

Their neurobiological difference linked to dysfunction of the neurotransmitter dopamine makes continuous stillness and focus almost impossible, and quite apart from the negative effect this has on their own learning, they disturb all the others around them. Often the affected children recognise what is happening but cannot take steps to control their actions. When a question is asked, children with ADHD may be overwhelmed by a number of answers and blurt out their chosen one, often without waiting for the question to be completed. Then the other children hoot with scorn. A potential source of bullying is born, and often taunts about what was said can be carried into the playground and used again, for bullying is relentless.

It is important that teachers understand that children with a genuine problem (not just naughty ones who do not want to do as they are told) have difficulties that frustrate them as well as their teachers and parents. They want to be still and concentrate but something in their make-up defeats them. While teachers want the children to focus and ignore distracters in the environment, it is these very items that fascinate them and urge them to move. They also feel their emotions so strongly that thwarting them can cause them to overreact, even hitting out, although they know that is wrong. So, they become known as bullies when it is really frustration that prompts such actions.

Bullying children can find many ways to set children with ADHD on edge while assuming innocence themselves. It is not hard to see how thinking and learning and the children's self-esteem are all affected.

But why should this happen?

The brain protects the mind–body link. Its main function is to keep the organism (of which it is a part) safe and well. And so it continuously scans the environment for stimulation. In response to stimulation, the brain creates urges that demand to be satisfied. If the stimulus is falling blood sugar, the urge will be hunger and a search for food. If the stimulus is wanting to go home or go out to socialise, then the urges are similarly accompanied by a feeling of emptiness that needs to be filled. This triggers the action that will satisfy the craving. Carrying out the action, for example cooking a meal or learning something new or climbing a mountain or finishing a piece of work, should be rewarded by positive feelings of pleasure and fulfilment.

So, when things work fluently there is a process of

Stimulus ⇒ urge ⇒ action ⇒ satisfaction

Sometimes that process breaks down. Either the urges lose their potency to prompt the action, as is the case in ADD, where the children appear to lack the motivation to keep learning, or the actions themselves do not lead to fulfilment or satisfaction. That is what is happening in children with ADHD. The insistent demands of the body make them move to seek out new stimuli, yet often the movement does not produce the reward that is sought. Feelings of satisfaction elude the child, who then has to keep moving to search out a new source of fulfilment. Such children are often blamed for behaviour they simply cannot help.

Yet children with this disorder can often concentrate for a short time. One child, asked why he didn't concentrate like that all the time, replied:

> Well, I can force myself to be still if something really interests me but then I feel this surge of energy and I've got to move. If I bottle it up too long, I just have to lock myself in the toilet and let off steam. But then people think I'm strange. Other kids just see the

strange bits and don't look underneath to find me. When I tried to explain, they just made loud whistling noises. It's so hurtful – and I do care. It makes me cry.

One of the successful strategies schools have used is to provide sunshine rooms. These are spaces where children can go if they feel these urges building up. Often, knowing that this facility is available helps the children to keep control. Understanding that this may ease at adolescence when the frontal cortex of the brain is stimulated to give more control can offer some comfort to parents, but if the child is only 4 or 5, it can be a long time to wait.

A particularly nasty type of bullying occurs when children without these difficulties stir up the children with ADHD and then retreat to enjoy the fracas. This is why when teachers record incidents, they should also note 'who was there', and if the same names appear in several instances, then a clue to the cause of the episode might just be revealed.

Poor planning, sequencing and organising competences (part of dyspraxia, dyslexia, ADD, ADHD and autism)

One of the pervasive differences in several additional needs conditions is poor organisation and planning. Could this difficulty contribute to children being bullied? Dane, a Year 3/4 teacher, explains:

> What drives me mad is when children can't organise themselves or their belongings. Every day they have the wrong books and no PE kit, and letters home lie at the bottom of their bags till they disintegrate. Then parents get ratty. 'Why aren't we informed?' they'll cry, when I have sent letters more than once. Sometimes I avoid making changes in routines in the day because I know that will cause stress, but that's hard on the ones who can cope. They tell me they are bored by everything being so predictable. Sometimes the class even misses an extra time to go to the hall because getting some of them undressed and dressed again is a nightmare. And some of the children will go out of their way to make things worse. They'll hide Tom's shoes or empty his bag on the floor and he is left distressed or aggressive. Maybe that sounds like horseplay but to Tom and to me it's bullying. They do things like that when I'm busy with other children. I know who is responsible but it's hard to prove anything! Why do children looking on not identify and openly reject these horrid ones?

Why do they think it's telling tales rather than supporting the needy ones? But on the other hand, why are the children who are disorganised, like this? They are always getting into hot water – it's always the same ones, and because these children look just like the others, busy people, admittedly including me, get so impatient. I try not to sigh, but it's so hard.

Thinking, planning and organising take place in the pre-frontal cortex of the brain, where the working memory also resides. Memorising is necessary to facilitate planning ahead. To plan, children have to reflect on what went before, then they have to amend that to suit a new context. If they cannot remember, then planning and organising are affected too. This is part of many special needs conditions and can affect children who are very intelligent. They become frustrated and angry and can lash out, hitting those who chide them. Then they are the ones who are labelled bullies.

Dyslexia

Jan is a nursery nurse who reflects on her school life with bitterness:

I was 14 before I was diagnosed with dyslexia, and no one at home could understand why I was always in the bottom groups for reading and spelling when I was good at subjects like drama and art, and in the school productions I could learn long speeches by heart. But they didn't know enough about the education system to challenge the teachers. I'm not sure the teachers knew what was wrong or how to help either, for they just shook their heads. I soon lost all confidence in myself and left school as soon as I could because at 14 I had too much ground to make up. I love my nursery nurse role with the children but it took years of evening classes and I know I could have achieved even more if I had had an earlier diagnosis.

Jan made a critically important point. 'Bullying is not just what people do – it's what they don't do. Leaving me to struggle was far more painful than stealing my books or the other kids telling me I was thick.'
Dyslexia has many forms and different causes that impact more or less severely on a child's competence in reading and spelling. Unfortunately, because so much school learning depends on those skills, children who are of even above average intelligence can see themselves

as stupid. One form of dyslexia is caused by a particular brain module failing to fire. Carter (2000) explains that PET scans taken when people with dyslexia were carrying out reading tasks showed that their language processing areas failed to work in concert. In non-dyslexics the language areas with a spot between them called the insula fired together. The insula acts as a bridge enabling the areas to work in unison. In those with dyslexia, the insula did not fire and so the language areas worked singly rather than being orchestrated to work together.

Peer (2004) in her Ph.D. thesis, 'Otitis media: a new diagnosis in dyslexia', ascertains that some children with poor reading and spelling skills have inadequate discriminatory hearing. While they are not deaf, they lack the ability to differentiate between sounds, for example between b, p, q and d. So, they cannot sound out words in their heads accurately, which obviously hampers their language skills. Surely this is something that should be checked at nursery?

Whatever the cause and whatever the difficulty, children with learning differences can be bullied by putting them in a class group that does not match their usually average or above average level of intelligence. Disguising streaming by naming groups triangles or foxes fools no one, least of all the children themselves. Perhaps the system of streaming children is inherently built on bullying? Some will argue that ability groups are the most efficient way to teach, but how can a bright child placed in the bottom group because of a lack of accurate diagnosis stay motivated to learn?

Gifted and talented children

And what of children identified as being gifted and talented? Surely their abilities and skills must take them out of the group of children with learning difficulties/disabilities/differences? In the past, children with dyspraxia, dyslexia and ADD or ADHD were named as having 'specific learning difficulties', which meant that their overall achievement was marred by a 'surprising downside in one developmental domain given their intellectual level' (Macintyre and Deponio 2003). Today, however, some gifted and talented children are found to have aspects of autism, more usually called Asperger's syndrome. They are high intellectual achievers, usually in one area such as memorising factual information or being gifted artists or mathematicians, but have the social and communication difficulties that distinguish children on the spectrum. Within this group are the mono-savants such as Kim Peake. To quote Kim's father, 'He can read one page of a book with one eye, the other with the other in 30 seconds and he never forgets anything he has ever read.' His encyclopedic memory made him the stimulus for the movie *Rainman*. Children like this with spectacular intellectual gifts like these are often isolated because of their difficulties with peer-group interaction and their obsessive interests. Their high achievement can also cause others to resent their ability and possibly encourage bullying.

Many high achievers are bullied at school. Their achievements are significantly different from those of other children. Parents often explain that this giftedness is innate, something the children are born with. Often they say, 'We don't know where it's come from.' Just occasionally, when the restlessness of these children gives them no peace ('Marie is never content, she always has to be on the go and we don't have the resources or the time to allow her to fulfil the challenges she sets'), they may wish that for a time their child 'could be an ordinary girl or boy'. The children's language is of a different quality and often they find it more satisfying to relate to adults. Their interests may be beyond the scope of the school to provide resources. Their gifts can also be resented by the other children and their parents. Their skills can cause them to be left out of games and other activities, and so gifted and talented children will sometimes deny their gifts, often getting answers wrong just to be one of the crowd.

Children who are talented in sports may be less prone to bullying because the other children can appreciate the vast amount of dedication and training that leads to their achievement. These others may also be pleased to reflect in the achievement if this brings kudos to them or the school. However, the isolate nature of training for some sports means that talented children can find it hard to make and sustain friendships too.

Does giving children a label help prevent them being bullied?

Many parents and professional are reluctant to send the children for a formal diagnosis of either difficulties or talents in the early years. (This diagnosis must be made by an experienced psychologist, as the co-occurrence of symptoms across conditions and the lack of boundaries between those who have a condition and those who are free of it are not clearly defined.) Nursery and school professionals understand that a surge in myelin within the brain around 6 years of age may reduce some difficulties, so they are reluctant to diagnose specific conditions before that time. Early years practitioners, however, can help the accuracy of any decision if they collect evidence of what the children can and cannot do in familiar surroundings and share this with those who make the diagnosis. A full picture, ideally with video snippets showing the children's movement patterns or pieces of their work, is always helpful, perhaps even essential if misdiagnoses are to be avoided.

Carol and Jack were parents who fiercely rejected the idea of giving their son a label. They asked:

> Why should he be called dyspraxic and dyslexic? Children can have chickenpox and no one would dream of calling them chickenpox children. There are all sorts of negative connotations attached to special needs labels. If a child has a label, then teachers expect them to fail at certain things; their expectations are lower, and that's not what we want for our son.

While this is totally understandable, there may be downsides to any delay. Many children with difficulties speak of the relief when they get a label, 'because for the first time we realise that not being able to do the things others do is not our fault'.

Listen to Sandy, a 7-year-old boy with dyspraxia/developmental coordination disorder (DCD). Sandy explains:

> When I was told what was wrong, it was like a huge weight being lifted off my shoulders. It wasn't the best news to be told that although physiotherapy would help, I'd always have DCD, but I knew it wouldn't get worse and, best of all, the family could stop blaming me for being clumsy. It was especially good to be told it was an inherited condition. This means I can ask, 'Whose fault is it anyway?' And when kids at school tell me off I can say, 'I've got DCD – you try to wear boxing gloves to do your writing and see how you get on. I bet it would be worse than mine.' Once I had a label, my teacher explained DCD to the class and that made them more patient. It's not knowing what's afoot that causes most of the upset. Now I am much more relaxed with my friends and my parents too.

Once a formal diagnosis has been made, the children should have extra support. They then learn that programmes of support can reduce their problems and that any who continue to bully do so in the knowledge that their actions will be seen as despicable.

While many learning differences are difficult to diagnose, often leading to parents being confused when their child is told he or she has a different condition from that diagnosed for another with apparently the same cluster of difficulties, more disabling conditions have features that make diagnosis clear. Are these children bullied?

Cerebral palsy

Listen to Marie and Ken, whose 10-year-old daughter Ashley has cerebral palsy:

> Ashley is quite severely affected by her cerebral palsy. She has very poor muscle tone so all her motor milestones are delayed. But that doesn't mean she can't make progress. One day she will be able to stand without her walking frame, I'm sure, although she'll always need her wheelchair and a substantial amount of support. Generally she is low-toned but occasionally her muscles go taut or her arms can flail around. But this passes, and as she gains control, that will improve. Cerebral palsy doesn't get worse, as some progressive disabilities do, so we are always positive, looking out for signs that she is getting stronger. We celebrate things she can do rather than despair about those she can't. We've learned this. When she was diagnosed at birth we despaired – it was terrible, but you have to get through that. Can she learn things? Yes, she can. Like her movement, progress can be slow but hey, what's the rush, God made plenty of time. She'll get there, I know she will.

But was she ever bullied? Ken was ready for this question:

> Well, thankfully when she was little, Ashley didn't realise how unkind people could be and we were able to explain why she was different before that happened. When adults stared, and believe me they did, we said things like, 'That lady would like to have your chair – she has to carry her shopping' and we would turn the chair away from inquisitive eyes. Often Ashley wasn't hurt but we were. No one came up and chatted to Ashley, they spoke over her and asked us if she could understand. She did understand, although she couldn't reply. On the whole, children were better. We asked neighbours' children in to play so that she could have some normal life and they would play around her. One day Ashley was made the queen in her throne. I doubt if she really understood but she loved the children and one girl told me she had written about Ashley for her class lesson. But not all children are like that. We were shopping one day when a gang of boys

about 10 years old shouted, 'Are you a spastic, then?' I shouted
back, 'She's not a horrible bully, anyway, so that's better than you.'
On reflection I thought it would have been better to ignore them.
It's bad enough being bullied yourself but when it happens to a
fragile child you ask, 'Can anything be worse?' We have to watch
other children running around and we wonder, 'what if . . .' but
then we pull ourselves together and are thankful that Ashley will
never be a nasty child like these boys.

Marie and Ken explained that cerebral palsy was caused by a hazard
that had affected Ashley's development in the womb. Her brain was
unable to send the correct signals to her muscles, so her posture and
movement – that is, her balance, coordination and control – were affected.
They were sure that Ashley's physiotherapy and listening therapy would
enable her to gain skills, although she would always need care.

A final word from the parents:

> We do the best we can to keep her happy and in a way we are
> lucky in that we can protect her from unkind people. But as she
> grows she is getting harder to lift and dress. We have to turn her
> during the night and sometimes we get very tired. Many people
> are kind but others knock us back by not knowing what to say,
> even crossing the road to avoid us. You wouldn't think people
> would bully a child in a chair, but they do.

Allergies

It may at first sight seem strange to include children with allergies in a
chapter on special needs conditions, but the effect of different allergies
can be devastating, even life-threatening, and they place a fearsome
responsibility on professionals in schools. As the number of children
with allergies is increasing in line with other additional needs, the effects
of keeping the children safe impact on the other children, as restrictions
limit their experiences too. This can be a source of bullying.

Listen to Laura, whose son Andrew had a peanut and soya allergy.
She explained:

> Having a child with these allergies is very frightening. To out-
> siders it sounds easy – he just doesn't get peanuts or Chinese
> meals. But traces of nuts are found in unrefined oils and they are
> in hundreds of other foods. So, we have to be vigilant every day,
> for even a small amount can cause a reaction.

Debbie, a teaching assistant who was preparing to take responsibility for Andrew, asked, 'What do I do if I suspect he is in trouble?' Laura replied:

> Well, Andrew is less severely affected than some children who go into anaphylactic shock, which is life-threatening, but his lips swell and he can develop difficulty breathing and swallowing. So far this has happened gradually but we worry that reactions could be immediate and severe. We are hoping he'll grow out of it but as yet he is very prone to these triggers. When Andrew comes to school, the environment has to be absolutely free of these allergens, for even sitting next to a child who has eaten peanuts in the playground can affect him. If you see his lips swelling then immediately get an ambulance and tell the paramedics it's possibly anaphylactic shock. Get them first and then phone me.

Debbie was given reading material and training in using an epipen and she was constantly vigilant about allergens. Unfortunately, the necessary limitations caused grumbling and even bullying. One example occurred when parents were asked not to bring any baking into school and to avoid any nut- or soya-related foodstuffs in lunch boxes. Sarah, whose birthday was imminent, was devastated because the school had always welcomed contributions of food for the birthday child's party. Some parents were disgruntled too, as they enjoyed being part of the scene. Andrew was told he 'wouldn't be invited to a party at my house' and 'if it wasn't for you we could have had a real birthday tea'. He was told he had spoiled everything. Bullying can take many forms. Andrew would always need the courage to make his allergies known and he had to learn to cope with harsh responses.

Debbie was anxious to know how common allergies were and what they were so that she could prepare the kitchen in advance of Andrew's arrival and be aware of difficulties a subsequent child might have. The Allergy Awareness Group (2007) explain that there are a handful of foods that are to blame for 90 per cent of allergies. They are known as 'the big 8'. They are milk, peanuts (groundnuts) and nuts from trees, eggs, soya, fish and shellfish, citrus fruit, and wheat. Some people with a peanut allergy are also allergic to green beans and peas, even lupins, as these contain allergens similar to those associated with peanuts. So, whether other children like it or not, the setting, even the garden, has to be carefully prepared for children with allergies. And all staff have to know the immediate drill if preparations fail!

As the numbers of children with difficulties are increasing, the demands on staff multiply too. Could insisting that staff cope without sufficient training, taking their remit well beyond its original limit, be a form of bullying? Perhaps it is!

3 Some important questions about communicating with parents

Question 1: How easy it is to talk with parents about bullying?

When staff in nurseries and schools were asked about communicating with parents, some, especially those in the early years settings, immediately claimed that their relationship was such that they could broach any issue, even bullying. 'This is because parents come into the nursery regularly and we become friends. Sometimes we get to know whole families so we build up trust and know that everyone is doing their best for each child.' Others were much less confident that topics such as bullying could be discussed openly. 'It's different if you are talking about behaviour at a general level,' explained Rhana, 'but when it gets personal, involving their child, when you are trying to find the words to say that there is a problem, it's a different story.'

Jack added another dimension to the discussion. He explained:

> When you ask parents to come into school, the balance of power is skewed. Even if they don't know what you want to discuss, they suspect something is wrong and they expect to be blamed for whatever it is. So, from the start they are on the defensive. It's an echo of the bully–victim scenario and it needs more than a cup of tea to dispel this atmosphere and relax them . . . and us, because we feel very apprehensive too.

Mandeep added:

> There are times when I would like to say to the parents, 'you are bullying me. I am doing my best for your child but you are making comments in front of other parents, saying that we are not doing a good job. That is so hurtful and so untrue.' Some parents tell me they are paying for their child not to get a scratch so if that

happens, they say there must be bullying and we are not doing our job. They are quite prepared to complain to health and safety. So, if we want to keep our jobs, we can't answer back. Sometimes I am shaking with nerves when I see them coming in. It's so unfair because we all work so hard and really care for the children.

But I have to admit that most parents are lovely and they agree that if their child gets a bump or falls down in the garden, then that's part of growing up, part of childhood, it needn't be anything to do with bullying at all. But there are parents who fear bullying so much that they forget that minor bumps can happen just as easily at home. They distort what really happens. If I could afford it, I would tell them to keep their child at home if they are not pleased. It's always our fault. Their child is never to blame.

Question 2: So are there techniques to reduce the likelihood of any friction between parents and staff?

Deb, a school manager, explains:

> The important thing is to be calm. You must give yourselves time to prepare your approach and follow the procedures set out in the school policy to the letter. After all, the parents may not know that their child is being bullied or that you have been trying to prevent their child bullying others. It's best to assume that this will be a new and particularly unwelcome message. You can tell the parents that it is school policy to confront any potential problems immediately so that together you can discuss the best ways to solve them. Surely they must agree to that?

Pippa explained her way:

> First of all I explain how well the children are doing at whatever they are best at. Then as sensitively and positively as I can I ask if their child had been upset in any way, because 'just recently your child's behaviour has been causing the staff some concern and we want to help'. When you listen to the parents, you get an insight into what's been happening at home, and this can explain a lot. In fact, sometimes when I hear what has been going on I wonder how children cope as well as they do.

Asked to elaborate on this, she added:

Well, when you meet parents for the first time, you tend to make assumptions according to how they speak about their child and how they dress, and on that basis you think their child will be all right or need extra support. But these surface things can hide stresses and strains in the family that can explain why a child is unhappy. One Mum blurted out that she had had daily hospital visits, and because she didn't want Sean to see his Dad all wired up with tubes, he had been looked after by different neighbours on a daily basis. Sometimes she couldn't get home when she had promised, and when she did, she was on edge and found herself snapping at Sean. Distraught, she explained that 'things are going from bad to worse'. Not understanding the cause, Sean resented his mother's unexplained absence and showed this through being extra demanding when she was there. This carried on at school, and of course the child couldn't explain because he didn't know what was going on.

Pippa had explained that understanding the whole context was the key to building sound relationships with the parents. She also wanted to emphasise that

> even when a child has been driving you mad, there's no use meeting the parents when you are angry and emotional. If you take time to find out what's caused the change in a child, things calm down and you are not left feeling you could have done more to help. If you go in with all guns blazing, that just makes the parents think that you are the bully, not their child!

Asked to give some concise advice to other practitioners, the group particularly interested in promoting parental inclusion produced this list:

- Be calm; welcome the parents with a smile because they will be anxious, too.
- Assume the parents don't know that their child has been behaving inappropriately and that the news will be a nasty shock.
- Show the parents that you respect them and their child.
- Stress that you want to work with them to support their child.
- Avoid telephone conversations; you need privacy and time to talk about the problem.
- Prepare your approach beforehand. Anticipate what could be said and think through possible responses. If you write brief notes, then

you can remind yourself of key points. Sometimes discussions go off at a tangent, and then you miss something important.

- Begin with positive statements. If you feel tentative or if you don't know the parents well, ask a senior member of staff to be present. In fact, it is good policy to have a second member of staff in the room. They can ease the pressure and help everyone keep calm.

- Assure the parents that disclosures will be kept confidential (but only if that is possible).

Question 3: What happens if parents refuse to accept the school's assessment that their child is bullying another one or if they blame the school? If the school is told, 'He doesn't behave like that at home, it must be your fault.' What is the answer to that?

Rhana volunteered an answer from her experience:

At my last pre-school there was one boy who just bulldozed his way around. He would not be persuaded to settle, and when we restrained him from fighting, he would shout and swear. He could always find outlets for his mischief and sometimes we had to smile. One day he pretended to smoke the bread sticks we had for snack. He was just copying what he saw at home. We knew his parents were smokers. Then the others joined in a soon we had a whole group of 'smoking' children! But when one boy tried to copy, he snatched his stick away and began poking him with it – really as hard as he could. So, of course, that had to be stopped. Spitting and shouts of 'you're not allowed to touch me' followed, and the upset was terrible. You can't ignore a child in a frenzy. He was kicking and biting and everyone was traumatised. But we had to restrain him for his own sake and to keep the other children safe.

That was just one incident, but the other staff were then on alert, waiting for him to explode again. Some children were beginning to copy his increasingly aggressive behaviour; others were afraid of him, especially the boy he had hurt, and the atmosphere was changing. So, we asked his parents to come in for a chat. I thought this would sort things out but it didn't turn out like that. In the parents' eyes he could not possibly behave badly and they suggested that another boy was the root of the trouble. 'Sort *him* out,' they insisted, 'and my boy won't have to watch his back all the time. That boy is a troublemaker at home and all the neighbours know it, so don't blame our son.' Obviously they were going to share their perception of what had gone on in school at home. It was all downhill from then on. A real disaster.

Question 4: So what can professionals do?

- Be sure you don't get involved in mentioning another child's name (even that of the victim) because the parents can contact them and claim that 'you said . . .'. Confidentiality has to be the key word.
- Keep a diary noting episodes of the bullying tactics the child used. Record when they occurred, how long they lasted, who was involved and who was looking on; how the difficulty was resolved, if it was; and how the affected children interacted thereafter.
- If parents appear volatile, then be aware that you could make life worse for the child at home. The child may be copying the parents' behaviour or their instructions to 'stand up for yourself'. Or they may go home and punish the child. That would be much worse.
- Try to make parents recognise that their responsibility for the child's behaviour does not stop at the school door. Share the school rules if they will listen. If not, provide a copy for them to take home. Explain that these rules have to be in place in a setting where there are many children. This prevents parents feeling that you are criticising their parenting skills.
- Inform the parents that the school will keep a record of incidents to help children think twice before bullying again. However, good behaviour will also be recorded, so that labels do not stick.

Needless to say, any records have to be totally confidential and carefully dated. A score of 1–10 can quickly record the severity of any happening. (The allocation of incidents to numbers could be discussed at a staff meeting.) Then, if repetition occurs, there is evidence rather than hearsay to share with the parents. The school personnel who take responsibility for the bullying policy should also give their approval to and oversee such a scheme, or suggest an alternative that they prefer.

Question 5: But what if the child is a victim – how do you explain that to parents?

According to Lucy, explaining to parents that their child is a victim is really difficult, but sometimes there is a child that just doesn't seem to fit in. Sometimes it's easy to see why e.g. if they grizzle all the time and moan 'someone's bothering me' just to get attention or if they do things that upset the others. Often they trail around and despite all the resources they don't seem able to make a choice and settle. Very occasionally there is an unhappy child because the others won't include them and asking children to let them play doesn't always work. On the other hand there are times when a child is picked on and there doesn't seem to be any reason at all.

Asked what the staff did then, Lucy continued:

Well, we have to react to the individual context. We try to support the child by suggesting things he would like to do, but we have to be careful that we don't prevent other children approaching. It's interesting though that sometimes the parents tell us what their children say about their time here and these descriptions can be very different from what actually happens. We set up a meeting because we were so concerned that one girl was not managing to be included or even make a friend, but when the parents came in they told us how popular she was and how she enjoyed playing with the others. That solved one aspect but as we were taken aback and couldn't disillusion them, we didn't tackle the real problem.

'Occasionally,' added Graham,

we just have to keep two children apart. Different personalities can mean conflict and we have to be sure no one gets hurt. We take time to build the children's confidence separately and then try to involve them together in an activity that they both enjoy. But we are always ready to intervene when things don't work out.

Question 6: How do you approach the topic of bullying in a primary setting?

Primary headteacher Myra explains:

At the start of the year we invite all the parents to an evening session to set out our stall. We usually begin by explaining any differences in the curriculum in the new session and we explain how we support children who find the transition difficult. That often prompts a parent to ask about our behaviour policy and what happens when a child transgresses our rules. All the talk is general at this stage. I tell the parents that time for individual interviews will be arranged with each child's class teacher and watch some of them switch off! It's amazing how self-centred some parents are.

The meeting usually starts off with discussions about how we deal with requests to take the children out of school for dentists and term-time holidays and things like that, but someone is sure to ask about how we cope with pupils who disrupt the learning for others. Many parents see the policy of inclusion as detrimental to their child's education and they need to understand the benefits that accrue for all of the children. They explain that children with learning differences take up too much of the teacher's attention and the discipline and the curriculum suffer. They don't want disruptive or aggressive children in class. That kind of observation often leads into explaining the school policy on bullying. Or if there has been a spate of bullying I am up front about it and assure parents we know it has gone on, and explain that the school policy outlines the steps we take to combat it.

Question 7: Do you circulate copies of the policy?

Myra continues:

So far, because until quite recently it seemed unnecessary as well as expensive, we didn't do that. We just alerted parents that there was a copy in the office for them to study. Also we didn't want to make it public that some of our parents can't read English too well. But I assured them that we take bullying and any poor behaviour very seriously and that every child is entitled to be free of worry so that they can benefit from their time in school.

I also reassure parents that education has been concerned about bullying for some time. It's not a new idea. In fact I show them an excerpt from the 1993 Department for Education and Science Guidelines. This states, 'The role of the school is to provide the highest standard of education for all its pupils. A stable, secure environment is an essential requirement to achieve this goal. Bullying behaviour, by its very nature, undermines the quality of education and imposes psychological damage. As such it is an issue that must be positively and firmly addressed through a range of school based strategies through which all members of the school community are enabled to act effectively in dealing with this behaviour.'

Question 8: In everyday language, what do you say to parents?

I offer this advice:

- It is important to keep a sense of balance in any talk of bullying, for many children will go right through school without any need to confront the issue at all.
- So, parents should not be overly concerned, especially as all members of staff are totally committed to keeping all our children safe and happy.
- If unacceptable behaviour or bullying should arise, there is a school policy, and school procedures are followed carefully.
- If you are concerned, contact the school. Do not delay, because it can be easier to resolve disputes before things escalate.

Let's listen to the parents now and hear their concerns.

Question 9: How would we know if our child is being bullied?

The advice listed by practitioners for parents of younger children was:

- Notice any changing patterns in the child's play, or attitude to activities. Children often act out what is happening during their day. So, mothering a doll might be replaced by smacking it; favourite toys may be rejected; toys can even be destroyed because they belong to childhood. The child may have been told he or she is a baby and this is one way of dealing with resentment.
- Look out for regression to earlier stages of development, such as clinging on to the parent or refusing to let an adult out of sight; or thumb sucking or rocking or wet pants. These are all signs of distress.
- Notice if your child is no longer invited to parties or other social events.
- Keep an eye on younger siblings because your child may begin to bully them. This is because a victim may react by becoming a bully.

- Notice if your child doesn't want to prepare for 'news time' or if there are any signs of distress when school is mentioned.

And for older children, signs to note could be:

- Your child may become reluctant to go to school or refuse to walk unaccompanied to school when they have done so before without complaint.
- Children may complain of illness, particularly headaches or sore tummies, but these complaints improve once the school day has begun and absence is guaranteed.
- Personal property may be damaged, for example books torn or a pencil case lost or lunch money 'mislaid'.
- Repeated requests for money are made and overreactions follow if these are refused.
- The child may have difficulty in sleeping and need adult company to settle, or may insist on a nightlight.
- The child may refuse to eat, especially at breakfast. This is especially likely if the source of bullying is the child's weight.
- When you ask, 'What's wrong?', the child says 'nothing' but is obviously worrying and/or depressed.
- Your child shows any kind of physical regression, such as bedwetting when dry nights have been the norm.
- The child has recurring bad dreams.
- A sociable child may become isolate, wanting to spend time alone in a bedroom.
- A happy child may become downcast and irritable, although this may be down to early adolescence. Mood swings and/or claims of worthlessness become the norm, for example 'I'll never be any good at anything . . . I'm not going to try.'
- Excessive activity may mask signs of depression. Also note any rocking or flapping hands. Alert the school or the doctor if this persists.
- The child shows changes in success at school, or poorer concentration, or lack of enthusiasm or motivation.
- Fewer texts, emails or phone calls arrive.
- The child shows sudden over-the-top interest in dress and persistent requests for IT equipment.
- The child has a sudden obsessional wish to collect things that have not stimulated interest before.

Question 10: What can parents do to try to prevent their child being bullied?

Parents can try to ensure:

- that their children arrive at school in time because late children can irritate the teacher and the other children by disrupting the lesson and having explanations repeated;
- that the children are clean and tidy and have appropriate clothing; that there are tissues available and that wiping one's nose on a sleeve is taboo!
- that their children are not overweight, for this can be a source of taunting which can lead to comfort eating that makes things worse;
- that the children have no habits that annoy the others, such as whingeing, demanding too much attention, eating noisily or chewing open-mouthed, even always calling out the correct answers before others have had time to think;
- that the children appreciate the different forms bullying can take;
- that their children know what to do, for example:

  - if they are bullied (for example, stay in a crowd, as bullies are less likely to pick on a person surrounded by others);
  - who to inform (for example, that their own teacher is the best first point of contact but there are others available such as the school nurse or a teaching assistant if this is easier);
  - where to go for support if no steps are taken (for example, the school office) or if they see someone else bullying;
  - how to comfort the victim and how to be a buddy (for example, in supporting the victim without becoming one).

Above all, the children should know that their parents or carers at home will act on their behalf.

Then, if the school alerts parents that their child is a victim, parents should talk to their child about bullying and let them know:

- that they are proud of them for having been open about the problem;
- that they have done the right thing in reporting it and it is the adults' job to sort it out;
- that bullying is not new – it happens to many children and the bully is the one at fault;
- that they, the parents, understand how devastating being bullied is and that they will always be there to support them;

- that they will work with the child to overcome the problem (for example, if the bully is disclosed, then avoidance strategies should be worked out until other measures are put in place);

If the child is very unhappy, consider a spell of home education. Another approach is to involve the child in a new activity that develops his or her interests. This can act as a healthy distraction, especially if groups of different children are present.

Question 11: If children have a learning difference, should the other children be told? Should any child be given a label?

Whether other children should be told about a child's learning difference is a very important question that totally depends on the parents' wishes. If a child has a specific difficulty or learning difference, parents and staff together can consider whether the other children should be told because then they know that any annoying behaviour, such as bumping and intruding on personal space, or getting out of their seat too much, is not the child's fault.

This knowledge may lead to a deeper level of understanding. Certainly children who know of a difficulty can be expected not to comment, or engage in any other form of unacceptable behaviour. Then, 'not knowing' is no longer a valid excuse. Most children can sympathise if they understand what is wrong, especially if they can see the child trying to cope with the disability.

Question 12: What about giving the bully a label?

Understandably, there is a reluctance to label nursery and primary-age children as bullies because labels can stick even when the child matures, the condition improves and the behaviour changes. The self-fulfilling prophecy has also to be carefully considered. If children named as bullies strive to live up to their labels, the situation is made worse. The plight of the victim is of paramount importance but the bully may be asking for help too.

Question 13: What is the best way for parents to contact the school?

The best way to contact the school is to write a letter explaining your concerns. A letter allows the staff time to absorb the contents and to reflect on the particular child's participation in school. It is helpful if the headteacher has permission to share the contents of the letter with other key members of staff, perhaps the special needs teacher or the playground supervisor, so that a fuller picture can be gained, but if parents prefer that this should not happen, they can be sure that all correspondence will be confidential. Parents should make their preference clear.

While this sounds quite straightforward – that is, the school identifying pupils and taking steps according to the school policy – the reality is complex. This is because an action that is seen as hurtful, bullying behaviour by one vulnerable child, who may well become demoralised by its effects, may be shrugged off by a more resilient child who can respond by laughing or retaliating in a cheerful, 'don't care' way and seem unaffected by the episode. Unfortunately, it is not easy for the vulnerable child to copy the more confident extrovert or follow the advice, 'stand up for yourself.' Indeed, it is doubtful that they should, because this may just cover up the unacceptable behaviour and do nothing to stop the bullies in their tracks.

The important thing is that parents share their concerns. Sometimes staff can show they are unjustified but with the new (Scottish) 3Rs being 'Respect, relationships and responsive care', the ethos of the school encourages parents to become a real part of their child's education and share in the ups and downs.

Shona, teaching 6-year-olds, explained:

> I was very surprised when one mum came in at break time. She was very anxious, almost distraught with worry. Nearly in tears, she explained that the children wouldn't let her son join in their playground games. He just stood alone and was miserable for much of the day. I took her to the window to watch and there was Alex in the midst of the crowd, thoroughly enjoying the break! Mum was amazed and so relieved. I could see thoughts passing through her head about how she had been made to feel anxious and how she had regularly compensated the child for his unhappy day. Coming in to share the concern had dispelled it, and fewer treats for Alex were in store!

But of course there are other times when staff have missed a child's unhappiness, for sometimes children smile to avoid admitting they are being bullied. All parents should contact the school immediately, because that prevents small incidents escalating. Every incident is taken seriously and procedures will be put in place. If these do not work, parents are invited into school to discuss other possibilities.

The key message is for parents to share any concerns early. If they are unfounded, that's great, and if not, there are steps to be taken to sort things out. No one wants to accept Byrne's (2003) claim that 'there will always be bullying'.

Question 14: What do you do if you find one child has been bullying another? How do you sort it out?

If one child has been bullying another, we try to diffuse the situation by calming the children down. If there is any physical hurt, then of course that is attended to straight away, and a distressed child is always given immediate care and kept busy with a favourite activity. We don't ask for immediate explanations. If it is aggression, however, we keep the children apart, give them a book to read and wait. We are following Paul Harris's (1992) sound advice. He explains that children even as young as 5 or 6 realise that the intensity of feeling does dissipate after the event. We find we get less emotional and probably more accurate descriptions of what occurred after a wait. In fact, some children have been know to come and say, 'We'll sort it out ourselves – it was just a spat. We're really friends.' We wish it were always like this, but there are always children who find it difficult to tolerate one another.

When this is the case, we use Edward de Bono's 'six thinking hats' approach (see the Appendix). We have some cardboard circles in different colours for hats. It is amazing, but just having these lightens and depersonalises the encounter. First of all the teacher, with a blue hat, asks each child to describe the event. Then the children describe the outcome; that is, 'what went on and what was the result?' After that, they take a green hat approach and answer the question, 'What else could you have done? Let's think of better ways.' Then they put on black hats and carefully consider, whether there could be any downsides to that new plan. This gives them a chance to think of any possible things they have not mentioned. If we resolve the situation, we say, 'We've sorted this out – let's all wear our happy yellow hats and be cheerful.' Sometimes when the children see that the issue is taken seriously, and they know they are being watched, that's enough. But if that doesn't work, we are into more solemn discussions, and mentions of sanctions have to be made.

Question 15: Do bullies usually act alone?

Bullies certainly can act alone, but more often the bullies want others to see the effect of their taunting. They want to be seen as the powerful ones. Some even relish being the bad guy. They perform for an audience. Sometimes the ringleader will insist that other children collaborate, and these children can be afraid to say 'no'. Then gangs are formed and the difficulty of getting accurate accounts of events escalates.

Question 16: Do victims ever 'ask for it?'

'No one should be forced to become someone different,' claimed Calum,

> but children need to understand how others see them and some-
> times they need simple strategies to help them change. Impulsive
> children can be advised, 'count to ten and think before you act';
> timid children can learn and repeat the mantra 'I can do it' and
> 'no one has the right to annoy me, I'll be strong today'. And
> children have to recognise that if they hit another, they are likely
> to be hit back, even harder, so it's wise to desist. And of course
> there are children who wind each other up, engage in fisticuffs
> and enjoy the fracas. All sorts and shades make life interesting
> but so hard to sort everything out.

Many teachers will sympathise and agree.

Question 17: What does the school do to support the victim?

Francis, teaching 7-year-olds, replied:

> The first thing is to assure the victims that they have our support
> and then we check vulnerable times, i.e. when the bullying
> occurred. Most often it's in the playground. We have a buddy
> system in place and that sometimes helps, for often responsible
> children know better than staff what is happening. We have to
> report upsets and traumas, but depending on the incident we try

to deal with it immediately, keeping the action low-key and not letting things escalate.

With the personal and social emphasis in the curriculum there is some time to discuss hypothetical issues but not nearly enough. We try to discuss different kinds of issues and give the children time to think of acceptable ways of coping in different taxing situations, for example if a gang of boys approached them, what would they do? This is real education, not schooling, but sadly this time can be taken up preparing for tests. But we do try to get the 'respect each other' message across. Unfortunately, the emphasis on test results leaves less able children vulnerable to more scorn.

Question 18: What does the school do to support the bully?

Francis continued:

> We have a school nurse who acts as a councillor and a first line of support for all of the children. Children go to Lyn with all sorts of worries or pains. They know that she won't tell anyone unless she has to, so they can be honest. She does keep a record of visits, and this can provide evidence of different victims pointing to the same bully. This record can also show sadistic bullies they are on the blacklist, but generally she stays positive. She'll say things like, 'I need to get a good report to sort your record out. How about it? Come and tell me when you've been kind and helpful.' So, the bullies know their improved behaviour will be noted too.

For strategies and examples of children's work on the topic of bullying, see Chapters 5 and 6.

Question 19: Is there a developmental reason why some children are prone to becoming bullies or victims?

Just as in every other aspect of development, children can mature at different rates, so empathy and altruism, the qualities that enable children to understand how others are feeling, and lead to their taking steps to support those in need, may emerge at different times.

Alternatively, the children may make a conscious decision to reject such feelings because other strategies get results more quickly.

Harris (1983) points out an interesting paradox. He explains that

> young children, irrespective of their family background realize that certain actions, particularly hurting or distressing another child, are wrong, but children vary a lot in their willingness or ability to abide by these ideals. They know intellectually that certain actions are unacceptable but find it harder to make their understanding guide their actions. When they can do this they have developed empathy and altruism.

Altruism is sometimes called prosocial behaviour. It is voluntary behaviour intended to benefit another person, while empathy is the ability to understand the feelings of another. Empathy is the forerunner of altruistic behaviour. Like all other behaviours, these change with age. In most children, prosocial behaviours seem to increase. Bee (1999) tells that generally primary-age children will donate more to a worthy cause than younger ones do, but, interestingly, comforting another child happens more in the younger groups, with primary-age children less willing to be involved. But those who do show more prosocial behaviour are those who regulate their own emotions well.

Question 20: Are there ways in which altruistic behaviour can be encouraged?

Eisenberg (1992) offers some advice. She claims that the following steps will promote the ethos that will allow children to develop altruism:

- Capitalise on the children's capacity for empathy through pointing out the emotional or physical implications for the person who was teased or hurt. Ask, 'How did that make (the hurt child) feel?'
- Create a loving, consistent family atmosphere. Children who are more firmly attached are more likely to be altruistic. Ideally, children are told they are loved as well as finding out through osmosis.
- Look for opportunities to praise the children for their altruistic behaviours, for example 'How kind you were to share your picnic.' Let them know that such behaviour is vitally important and that it is recognised. Give awards for kindness. For example, at school, let a kind child hang a leaf on the kindness tree at school, and at home, let the child have extra time to spend on a favourite activity.

- Provide rules to clarify helpful behaviour, for example 'Let's all help to tidy up' or 'We should all share with children who have less than we do.'
- Model thoughtful, respectful behaviour so that children see words in action.

But still differences occur. Harris observed 4-year-old children when their mother left them in a room with a younger sibling who was showing distress at her departure. Some children immediately left their own play to comfort the baby but others simply ignored the baby's cries. Could these differences be caused by the children's temperament?

Question 21: Does the child's temperament link to bullying behaviours? Are some children born bullies?

Mothers as well as researchers will support the theory that children are born with different temperaments. Some babies from the start are irritable and restless while others are placid and easier to nurture. Temperamental characteristics are sometimes displayed on a continuum, and it is claimed that they are relatively enduring, affecting the way children view their world. By nursery age, children with difficult temperaments are more likely to show heightened aggressiveness or other forms of behaviour problems, and these may persist. However, this trait can usually be ameliorated by supportive, consistent and loving parenting skills, particularly in the early years (Bee 1999). However, easily stressed or ultra-sensitive children are more vulnerable than those with a more placid temperament, especially if support is missing. One temperamental trait, particularly affecting bullying is:

resilience———vulnerability

Resilient children and vulnerable ones in the same situation will have very different perceptions of events. The resilient ones will concentrate on the fortunate or happier occurrences while the vulnerable ones will see the downsides and negatives. One sees the bag of sweets as half full and is happy, while the other considers it half empty and is sad. It is not difficult to observe that some children instinctively smile and draw others to them while others frown and repel overtures to play. This inherited difference can certainly affect children's social competence and popularity.

Question 22: How does temperament affect the bully and the victim?

Dane, head of the counselling service for a group of schools, explains:

> When we discuss the feelings of the victim after an episode of bullying, we try to make sure the bully appreciates the effect his behaviour has had. The bully has to empathise with the other child. But it's so difficult to know whether this has occurred. In a situation where blame is being applied, facial expressions are not spontaneous; they are likely to be controlled or even manipulated so that true feelings are suppressed. It is not always possible to know whether the children are paying lip service to an adult's entreaties or whether they genuinely are sorry for their deeds. Sometimes the child named as the victim can give a nervous smile and the bully misinterprets this and feels he has been tricked or if the victim has engineered the situation to get the so-called bully into trouble – and some children can connive to make this happen – then their body language doesn't match their words and the 'bully' can read this and silently vow to seek revenge.
>
> Or perhaps some children have not matured enough, because we aren't born altruistic, or perhaps they have not had the role models to show them how to behave? If the ability to appreciate the perspective of another person is absent, if the child has not developed what is known as a theory of mind, then a bully may have to offer comfort in a situation that to him is not distressing. So, 'say you are sorry' is just a panacea and the interchange has little real effect!

Question 23: After the discussion, what then?

The anti-bullying group were anxious to follow Harris's (1992) lead and wherever possible build their curriculum around social and emotional development. As a result, when unfortunate incidents occurred, we decided to be up front with the class because they know what's going on anyway. We say things like, 'OK, we've had an unhappy incident today but it's sorted out now.' Then we have to say whether the incident was serious and how it was dealt with. Or if it was the result of a misunderstanding, we say, 'it's no longer important and it is forgotten, for the people involved are friends now and working together well'. The children see how we try to be fair, listening to the bully and the victim equally, and we stress that we will do everything to help prevent further unhappiness. We endorse the mantra 'Everyone is working for this class to be the kindest in the school. Does everyone agree?' And generally – and thankfully – most children say that they do!'

4 Developing prosocial behaviour: understanding friendships

Jason, a 12-year-old being looked after by a family, wrote this poem.

Don't tell the other children
That I don't stay at home
Honest, it wasn't my fault
That I'm stuck here all alone.

My Mum was always poorly
My dad was off at sea
I have no caring aunties
So there was only me.

The social came along then
And thought I couldn't cope
My Mum told me to be brave
And never give up hope

I had to leave and go to care
The people there are kind,
My mum is being cared for too
She tells me not to mind

But it's not home to live like this
I'm angry and I'm sore
I don't want to live with someone else
We're not a family any more.

Jason, aged 12

Listen to Gil describing her experiences with her 'looked after children'. This is particularly relevant, as many 'looked after children' come from families that have ongoing problems. It does not suggest that these children will be bullies or victims but seeks to explain different factors such as lack of continuity, self-blame for marital discord, illness, poverty; that is, hardships that singly or together could contribute to children's lack of confidence and behavioural difficulties.

Gil explains her experience with Amy and Sharon:

I have had a 4-year-old little girl and her sister of 2 for over a year now, and they have just been reunited with their mum and dad, who previously had been unable to cope. Although information about the parents is very limited, I knew they had also been 'in care'. Perhaps this is why they seemed to accept, without any rancour or apparent dismay, that I would care for their children till they were able to have them back.

The two children were very different characters. Amy was strongly attached to Sharon, her little sister. She always looked out for her and would check that her bottle was ready and that the bath water was the right temperature, things like that. We felt that she had taken a great deal of responsibility for her at home. She was smiling and biddable, adjusted to her new surroundings easily and appeared self-contained and confident. The younger child was quite different. Possibly the age factor had something to do with it. She was very difficult to settle, at times defiant but at the same time endearing, and of course we knew that she had had too much change and disruption in her short life. She learned early that 'wery wery sorry' would melt our hearts, and it was difficult to establish boundaries when tantrums and destruction were the norm. Of course I became very fond of both the children and although I wanted the family to be reunited, I was devastated at the thought of losing them.

But when that time came, they seemed totally unconcerned. They just packed their case and left. Then I realised they hadn't bonded with me at all. Was this a survival mechanism against them being hurt? Or did they just not feel emotions? Or should we not expect children, even at that very young age, to bond with someone outside the family? I had tried to give them a good start but of course I realise now that my goals were very different to theirs. They had seemed to accept walking the dog and swim- ming with the neighbours' children and healthy snacks but seemed unconcerned at leaving all this. Maybe wall-to-wall tele- vision and takeaway meals were more attractive? Later I was able to talk with the parents informally and the mum explained that the children were in care again. Had they seemed upset at leaving home? 'Not at all,' Mum replied, 'I tell them it's another adventure! Why should they be upset? In fact they have a better time away from the quarrelling that goes on here. There's always somebody shouting – it's not the best place for kids.' I wondered, in view of the way these children lived, if this lack of bonding would be a good or a bad thing. If they didn't bond now, would this affect them building strong relationships later? Would it matter in the future? Or perhaps it was just me that had failed and they would be happier in another home?

Bonding and attachment

Gil raised the important issue of bonding. Over the years this has been a controversial issue, with early claims (Ainsworth 1973) of the immediacy of bonding and its importance in forming long-lasting relationships somewhat overset by counter-claims that while 'early bonding may have some short term effects, long term benefits are small or non-existent' (Myers 1984). The early claims that bonding happened immediately after birth led to changes in hospital practice, for example fathers being brought into the delivery room to share the first moments. And although most fathers reported this as being a positive experience, sadly Lewis (1986) found no correlation between having that experience and being more involved with continuous childcare.

Later research, however, denied the immediacy of bonding, and many parents who had to be separated from their baby, perhaps because of illness or prematurity, or others who were dismayed to feel no immediate bond, were comforted by the information that bonding could happen later, even much later when, say, the post-natal blues had passed. The early researchers were criticised for having too small a sample of children and having to rely on mothers' descriptions of their children's reactions. Beyond the timing debate, however, many close-knit families wholly dedicated to their children's well-being over the whole lifespan would support Ainsworth's stress on the worth and longevity of the bonding process. Bee (2004) explains that the critical ingredient in forming a bond is the opportunity to 'develop real mutuality – to practice the dance until both partners follow each other's lead smoothly and pleasurably'. The learning involved takes time and patience, and not all adults succeed.

Unfortunately, there are factors that act against attachments being formed. Depression in the mother is very significant, not only for delayed bonding but because many depressed parents see their children as being more problematic and are more critical of them even when outside observers can spot no negativity in their behaviour. Also, the parents' own attachments are important. Many pieces of research have found that insecure attachments in the parents within their own families means that they are less likely to bond successfully with their own children.

Where attachment has occurred, it is commonly agreed that, in social situations the children will use the mother as a base to explore and will be stressed by her absence. To try to find how children did react, Ainsworth (1973) devised a way of observing children when they were placed in what was called a 'strange situation'. In a room not previously known to the child, nine episodes that were videoed and analysed. They involved monitoring the children's reactions over a twenty-minute period, paying special heed to the moment when a stranger joined the mother (or the caregiver) and the infant, then again after a little time when the mother had left the room. Especial attention was paid to the reunions when the mother comforted the child. From this research Ainsworth determined a number of different attachment types. At the reunion there were,

- Babies who avoided proximity to the mother and gave her minimal greeting – if acknowledging her at all. Subsequently they would avoid gaze and so intentionally limit communication.
- Babies who showed distress at the mother's absence and who sought reassurance from her on her return.
- Babies who sought some contact but gave the impression of being ambivalent.
- Babies who showed a disorganised or disoriented pattern of behaviour.

Why were these observations important? It was mooted that assignment to each category could predict other aspects of development; in other words, the behaviour acted as a prognosis of future attitudes and behaviours. Oppenheim *et al.* (1988) claimed that

> secure attachment at 12 months correlated with the quality and sensitivity of mother–infant face-to-face interactions at 6–15 weeks, with curiosity and problem solving at age 2, with social competence at nursery at age 3 and with empathy and independence at age 5.

However, these results must be interpreted with caution. Different cultural practices (for example, mothers staying with or having separation periods from their very young children before the research took place and so ameliorating the newness of the research event or the babies' previous experiences of meeting strangers when their mum was present or absent) would have to be considered.

These examples show just how difficult it is to control all the outside influences when carrying out research with very young children, not least because their reactions can vary from day to day – even within the same day if they become tired or out of sorts. Also, parents' observations are likely to be biased; they see what they hope is there, and so skew the results.

Different studies have looked at separation anxiety in older children. The children were asked to look at pictures of separation experiences, such as a parent going away from a railway station with a suitcase, and to describe feelings (1) that the child in the picture would have, and (2) the ones they themselves they would have if that happened to them. Securely attached children acknowledged the anxiety of the experience but gave coping responses indicating that they had appropriate solutions to the problem, whereas insecure children denied the anxiety or only made suggestions that were not realistic or feasible.

Bonding with dad

Although generally most babies have more time and contact with their mother, studies show that fathers can be just as competent; they can fulfil a parenting role just as well as mothers (Bee 2004). However, the strength of the attachment can depend on how much time the dad is able or wishes to spend with the child and with the number of baby chores such as nappy changing he undertakes! This finding led to fathers in Sweden in particular having sabbaticals at home so that they could become securely attached.

Attachments beyond babyhood

By age 2 or 3, attachment behaviours become less visible. Toddlers have the intellectual skills to understand the caregivers' promise that they will return, so their separation anxiety wanes. So, in non-stressful situations the child can stray further and longer from the parents without distress. By age 4, children understand that the relationship between them and their parents continues even when they are apart, and gradually they come to realise that in being apart they can be cooperating in achieving a shared goal. This is why it is so important for parents to share planning: cognitively, children are ahead of being able to express their feelings. But if no time is taken to explain events to the child or if the child feels unwell, then regression to a younger way of behaving is common. Thankfully, understanding and support can ensure that this is a temporary relapse.

Listen to Lesley:

> By the time Emily was 4, I had to get back to work or I'd be too far behind to catch up with developments and new technology. It was lovely being at home full time but I needed to get back into the workplace. So, Emily went to the nursery I had carefully chosen, and I expected she would be happy there. But the staff told me she was distressed for most of the time. She wet her pants, cried with a sore tummy and then began to bite and kick the other children. I could hardly believe it, but when I went to collect her, she hit out at me as well. When the staff asked if I had explained what I was doing when she was at nursery, I was amazed. I had told her about the other children and the toys but hadn't thought she'd want to know where I was. When she calmed down and wailed, 'Why do you have to go away?', I explained how we needed money to buy her clothes and shoes. Eventually she worked out that she was 'working at the nursery to get shoes' and cooperated much more. She considered that both of us were working to achieve the same goals. If this hadn't happened, she could have been labelled a horrid child. Explaining in this detailed way was not something I would have thought about myself. I would have thought her too young to rationalise in this way. It shows the danger of underestimating your child!

Warmth, responsiveness and hostility in the home

Closely linked to bonding is the emotional tone of the home. 'Warmth' has been difficult to define or quantify, but, even intuitively, it is recognised that a home where affection permeates the day provides security and a sense of well-being. Not unexpectedly, research shows that children from this type of home are more securely attached in the first two years; they have higher self-esteem, show more empathy and altruistic behaviour; they are more sure of themselves and more able to sustain friendships. Warmth also makes children more amenable to guidance (Macdonald 1992). Within the home that emanates warmth, the parents are sure to show responsiveness to their child, and this skill in picking up children's signals in a positive, encouraging way is linked to cognitive development; that is, to the children having a higher IQ. Social and emotional benefits are described as children being more outgoing and more amenable to changes in routine. Bornstein (1989) claims that babies with responsive parents learn language more easily; these children have higher IQ scores and are more socially competent, and are less likely to indulge in damaging behaviour when they are older.

Given these advantages, it is not difficult to gauge the downsides for children brought up in a hostile environment and to understand why children are removed from abusive families. But why in an affluent, supposedly caring country such as the United Kingdom should more and more families encounter such difficulties? Palmer (2006: 13) explains that

> in the tumult of change, it is not surprising that parents have lost sight of age-old truths about child rearing. In the past, lore from the extended family, cultural and religious traditions were used as reference points, but for many families they have been swept away.

So, if social rules no longer provide guidance and if boundaries break down, does a sense of anomie or normlessness with no fixed expectations replace coherence and family cohesion?

Hostility

Have these changes led to increased hostility in some homes, and what would be the implications of children being raised in a hostile environment? Even a basic level of coolness can limit parent–child spontaneous communication and promote a wariness in children that influences their capacity to form relationships with their peers. More severe is continuous verbal and physical hostility. This leads to children becoming aggressive or delinquent or very withdrawn. Not having experienced respect, even being listened to, how can they interact respectfully with others? Physically abused children are more likely to suffer from depression and more serious social problems, and are more likely to retaliate physically in encounters where they are thwarted. Sexually abused children show a variety of disturbing behaviours from nightmares and separation anxiety to post-traumatic stress disorders, behaviour problems and low self-esteem. The severity of reactions is correlated with the length and severity of the abuse. Despite all this knowledge leading to educational programmes for parents and caregivers, and social workers and teachers having a much greater awareness of hidden abuse, it appears that society cannot find a way to eradicate it. Will these children, reacting to what they have seen or full of resentment because they recognise they have had a raw deal, be prone to becoming bullies?

But of course relationships are built on a dyad, or two-way encounters. Children influence their parents as well as the other way around. And with the increasing number of teenage pregnancies, some young, immature parents are ill-prepared to take on the responsibility of parenthood. One young mother explained:

> No one told me how hard it would be. There was no one to take a turn, all my money was needed for nappies and I couldn't stand being with her all the time and missing out on all the things teenagers do. I had had a baby to get someone to love me. But she didn't. She just cried and cried so I hit her.

How very sad is that?

But even with more experienced parents, the child's temperament can cause frictions within the family.

Children born with difficult temperaments

From the start, some children are more irritable and less responsive than others. If they grizzle for much of the day and fail to achieve a regular sleeping pattern, the dynamics of the household can be put under tremendous strain, especially if there other worrying factors such as poverty or getting work completed in time, or poor health to be considered. On top of that, friction between parents can arise if they disagree on how the child should be parented. If one changes the 'rules' in the absence of the other, then boundaries of expectation shift and the young child is left confused, not knowing whether praise or punishment will follow or whether the outcome will be the same or different for similar actions. The slightly older, more experienced child may play off one parent against the other – 'She said I could, so there!' Thus, conflicts and tensions fester. And because most parents avoid venting their distress on the child, they harangue each other. The child, although physically unharmed, is a witness to bullying behaviour. And as children's learning is at least partly based on imitation and modelling, the seeds of bullying are sown.

Bee (2004) explains that the temperament/docility of the first child is especially important because the parents have little experience; they will be stressed and exhausted, and if their child continues to be distressed, they may judge themselves as being inadequate parents. When their child's difficulties last through baby and toddlerhood and parents' expectations are still not being met, then the child may be blamed for the stress. Physical punishments can be meted out. The child wails more loudly still and the cycle of despair goes on. Relationships off to a poor start can take a long time to heal and the situation requires great tolerance on all sides.

Parenting styles

Baumrind's (1972) typology of parenting styles makes fascinating reading. She considers the four of the dimensions mentioned above. These are (1) warmth or nurturance, (2) levels of expectation or maturity demands, (3) the clarity and consistency of rules, and (4) the quality of communication between parents and child. She defined four parenting styles:

- The permissive style. This style is high in nurturance but low in maturity demands, control and communication.
- The authoritarian style. This style is high in control and maturity demands, but low in nurturance and communication.
- The authoritative style. This style is high in all four dimensions.
- The neglecting or uninvolved type. This style is low in all four dimensions.

What effect do parenting style have on the children and could lack of vital competences, either by omission or through the providing of unfortunate role models, promote bullying behaviour?

The permissive style

Children growing up with permissive parents tend to be lax in self-control. They do not readily take responsibility, and as they are used to a great deal of freedom, they can become aggressive when they have to obey someone else's rules. They tend to be immature because they have not been allocated tasks or been asked to conform to time limits.

They find it hard to anticipate the outcomes of actions because this has not been required.

The authoritarian style

Families using an authoritarian style use high levels of control and maturity demands, so the children must obey without demur and without conjuring up alternative ways of behaving. So, problem solving and skills of independence are less likely to be developed. Low levels of warmth and responsiveness are also associated with children doing less well academically and socially. When children are held down in the home, they may well react with impulsiveness or aggression once they taste freedom.

The authoritative style

The most positive style in terms of positive outcomes for all aspects of development, including relationships, emotional stability and intellectual development, is this authoritative style. Children have higher self-esteem because they are listened to with respect, and tasks are achievable with just the right amount of challenge. They are more independent but also more willing to be guided by parents. They are also more likely to show empathy to those less fortunate than themselves, and their actions will be guided by moral reasoning.

The neglecting or uninvolved style

In this style the parents adopt a laissez-faire attitude and provide only basic requirements in contact and nurturance. As a result, the children lack guidance and often make decisions about their education and welfare that bode ill for the future. They are more likely to experiment with drugs and feature more in the statistics on teenage pregnancies.

Quality of the living environment

In every society there are layers of advantage and disadvantage, and each has different access to resources. Naturally this affects the well-being of all family members. Stress builds up when parents cannot afford even a basic standard of comfort and a proper diet for themselves and their children. Undernourished mothers or those who take drugs to blot out the pain of the day are not providing the best first environment – that is, the womb – and as a result, their babies are smaller and more liable to be poorly, causing more worry and stress. Families tend to be larger, homes more crowded and children have all the restrictions of poverty. They lack the opportunities and the age-appropriate toys that more advantaged children have. And if the parents have not had educational opportunities themselves, how can they engage their children in intellectually stimulating activities? Perhaps it is not surprising that relatively deprived parents treat their children differently, being more liable to use the authoritarian parenting style.

The effect of divorce

Any change in the family structure will be accompanied by dislocation and stress. There are so many changes, such as the loss of one parent in the everyday family system, continuous conflict, sudden economic change and ongoing feelings of being betrayed. Almost inevitably there is disruption in the children's routine and much separation anxiety, especially if explanations have been sparse. Very unfortunately, and without any evidence, many children overtly or covertly blame themselves. For several years after a divorce, many children can be depressed and angry, and this affects both their schooling and their friendships. Their self-esteem suffers, and unless the divorce is amicable and extremely well managed, they may lose confidence in making and sustaining friendships throughout their junior schooldays (Palmer 2006). Custody issues can be acrimonious and long-lasting. Moreover, if one parent feels deprived or cheated, the children can end up being passed back and forward like parcels, shattering any continuity and security in their upbringing.

In the earliest years the children will sense the stress without understanding what is amiss; in the school years, does the fact that so many children have lived through disruption help at all? Do children discuss such things or do the very different variables encroaching on each couple prevent this? Would peer support be helpful? Could this even be the source of developing friendships? Attitudes towards divorce have changed as it has become more commonplace. Previously, marriage was regarded as a sacrament and a lifelong commitment but today, divorce in the United States is almost the norm, marriages falling apart when other priorities appear. And the United Kingdom is not far behind. Hetherington (1999) has charted the changes in the behaviour of the parent who stays. They typically show mood swings and have problems at work, possibly because they feel disoriented, or because work issues feel less significant amid their other traumas. Time pressures mean that their pattern of parenting changes, so that they do less well at monitoring their children's behaviour. Either the departing parent or the remaining one or both may over-indulge the child as compensation for the distress, and of course the child can react to this with gratitude, cynicism or complete rejection of the favours that have been bestowed.

From the literature on remarried families, it seems that the closer the parents appear to the children to be to each other, the more problems the children display. The opposite finding is the case for non-divorced families. There, parent closeness correlates with children's well-being. The timing between the first marriage breaking down and the second happening is a contributory factor. When a parent and children have been alone for some time, then the children can feel displaced by the new partner, who takes over roles held by the children since the split. Conflict is especially likely if, in the children's eyes, the remaining partner gives in too much to the new one; if, for example, new discipline measures seem to diminish the previous ways of awarding praise and sanctions.

In many parts of the world, extended rather than nuclear families are the norm. Several generations live together in the same household. Studies of children brought up like this claimed that in a crisis children were less dependent; they had fewer sleep problems; they had better levels of self-care. The best single predictor of these benefits was the child's grandmother. She was able to act as a buffer and her experience kept things in proportion. As more and more grandmothers in the United Kingdom are taking a huge role in their grandchildren's upbringing, perhaps these benefits will be found here too!

Making and sustaining friendships

Given that children come from a range of backgrounds where different parenting styles have been experienced, and where their own special blend of competences and difficulties make each child unique, how do they begin to make friends? And how important is it for children to have friends? Why should some children make friends easily while others are isolates?

Most children feel buffeted from bullying if they have a friend, but it can be difficult for adults to persuade children to make a friend with someone who is not their immediate choice. Pleas to 'let a certain child play' are rarely successful. So, how are friendships formed and what is it that can make some endure despite hardships and disruptions and family upsets?

When do children form friendships?

Children begin to show interest in other children as early as 6 months of age. They do not have the muscular control to do more than smile unless they are in close proximity, when they will 'investigate', perhaps pulling each other's hair or flailing arms in the general direction of the other. But by 14 months, children will play alongside one another, perhaps cooperating momentarily but most often side by side but with different toys. As long ago as 1932, Parten described this as parallel play – a term that has been used ever since. But by 18 months, children are more involved, chasing each other or imitating actions with toys. Their greater social awareness and cognitive development make this possible. And by 3 or 4 years they prefer to play with their peers rather than alone or with an adult. They even begin to share imaginative stories and fantasy play. Then there are opportunities for both aggressive and prosocial, altruistic behaviour.

Instrumental, verbal and hostile aggression

Most children show aggressive behaviour at some time. In the early years it is usually to procure some object of desire (i.e. instrumental aggression), rather than hostile aggression that houses the desire to hurt another person. But of course hostile aggression does occur, especially before children have the language to explain or make requests known. Impulsivity can play a part here. Young children tend to act before they think out the consequences of their actions. Generally the upset is short-lived and readily forgiven, belonging to the moment rather than casting a cloud over the future. As their verbal skills improve, most children replace hostile aggression with verbal aggression such as name calling or taunting, or they are usually positive and kind.

The decline in physical aggression mirrors the children's diminishing egocentrism and growing sociocentrism – that is, awareness of what it is like to be the recipient of hostility and hurt, along with the growing awareness that such behaviours are wrong. This will have been explained by parents and practitioners if it does not develop spontaneously.

Another important development in social awareness and the decline of physical aggression is the emergence of dominance hierarchies. As young as 3 or 4, children arrange themselves into pecking orders, seamlessly becoming leaders and followers. They know who will win disputes and who will lose. The children who do not wish to accept their place and who know they will not win are those who will find sly, more insidious ways, such as telling tales or whining, 'it's not fair', to achieve their goals. Aggression does not always follow frustration but it makes it more likely. Now simmering resentments do last, and the frustration may be vented some time after from the event that caused it. This leads to children becoming wary of those they suspect could pounce. This is the emergence of bullying behaviour and explains exclusions from nurseries when children are as young as 4.

Prosocial behaviours

Prosocial behaviours are intentional voluntary behaviours that are designed to help others. Such caring ways can be seen even in 2- or 3-year-olds, especially if they have warm, generous role models at home. When this involves some denial for themselves, such as a child offering another the only toy the child would really like for him- or herself, this is known as altruism. These behaviours change with age. The children are beginning to understand that other children have more or less than themselves, and they are also beginning to recognise the emotions of others, especially when they are needy.

Altruistic behaviour does increase with age as these awarenesses develop, seen when primary-age children are willing to give more to less fortunate children. Eisenberg (2002) found that children like this were more able to regulate their own emotions and were less liable to outbursts, or tantrums. He also offered guidance on how such competences could be nurtured:

1. Capitalise on the children's capacity for empathy. For example, immediately your child hits another, explain how that other child will feel. Eisenberg found this strategy most effective when it was not combined with physical punishment.
2. Create a loving and warm family climate. Express warmth towards your children for small acts. For example, you might say, 'When you helped me carry that, I was so pleased because I knew you were a kind boy.'
3. Provide clear rules or guidelines about helpful behaviour: 'We should always share with people who are not so lucky as we are' or 'Look out for someone who has no one to play with and let him join in.'
4. Ask children individually, 'How many helpful things did you do today?' And take time to listen. This is a strategy that works for 7- or

8-year-olds, and that is important, for this is the time when children are beginning to develop a global self-esteem.

5. Give the children responsibility for appropriate tasks and praise whenever they have been completed.

6. Above all, model altruistic behaviour, for children are likely to do what you do rather than what you say!

Social awareness and altruism help children subdue their own interests to sustain joint endeavours. This is at the root of sharing and following someone else's lead, part of the necessary cooperation to sustain friendships.

What influences friendship patterns in junior school children?

Children of age 5 or 6, who appreciate gender differences and recognise that these are permanent, now allocate certain kinds of behaviour to boys and girls. For a time, these rules are immutable, but then flexibility creeps in as experience tells that, for example, men can be nurses and women can drive buses. Yet at this time children become biased against those who are not like them – perhaps children of another race; those who speak another language; those who are obese. There seems to be segregation between 'those who are like us' and 'those who are different'. For the same reason, children from minority groups tend to gather together. The groups are trying to make sense of what is and what is not socially acceptable in their environment. The policy of inclusion was intended to reduce these biases, and certainly many schools report that all the children are mixing well. In 2008, perhaps some parents apportion negative differences more than their children do.

School-age children spend more time independently with their friends, gradually increasing the number of reciprocal friendships. Now friendships last longer; in junior schools, 'best friends' can last for a year and some for much longer, even into adulthood. School-age children are more open and supportive with their friends, yet they can be more critical too, and they have more conflicts (Hartup 1996a). When conflicts occur, however, they are more anxious to resolve them than when they fall out with non-friends. Boys' friendships appear to be more competitive, with the duo striving for dominance, while the girls spend more time nearer home in quieter pursuits.

Perhaps this explains why boys are seen to be more aggressive across cultures, or perhaps physical aggression is encouraged at home? Girls have a different means of expressing their aggression: they avoid the physical but use relational aggression; that is, they try to damage their victims' self-esteem.

Children who persist in using either physical or relational aggression are those who are named bullies. They have no empathy for their victim's pain or unhappiness. Olweus's (1995) studies do not support the claim that bullies are basically insecure children who have developed a tough exterior to cover their insecurities. He claims that 'Bullies have low levels of insecurity and anxiety'. And he proposes four child-rearing factors that could contribute to the development of bullying behaviour:

1. indifference and lack of warmth from the parent to the child in the early years;
2. lack of clear limits set on aggressive behaviour set by the parents;
3. the parents' use of physical punishment;
4. a difficult impulsive temperament in the child.

In other words, they match the descriptors of authoritarian and neglecting parenting styles described earlier.

Do these behaviours endure beyond junior school?

Unfortunately, there are long-term consequences of aggressive behaviour in children, possibly because the turmoil they have caused at school has caused them to be isolated or perhaps these early behaviours have cast them into a role that they are unable to discard. Longitudinal studies of aggressive children at 8 find they are aggressive at age 30, with many regressing further into criminal behaviour. And both boys and girls showed poorer advancement in their education. Their lack of social progress was inhibiting their cognitive gain. Swedish studies also showed that high levels of aggression at 4 or 5 years correlated highly with delinquency in early adulthood.

Such studies show the importance of early friendships and of supporting children who do not find it easy to make a friend. Explanations of the consequences of aggressive behaviour have to be understood by the aggressors when there is still time for them to make changes, and other children have to be encouraged to let them try, and to accept and praise their efforts. This is hard, but, given the consequences of not trying, it is the only way.

5 Understanding and enhancing self-esteem
Reforming the bullies and the victims

The sadistic bully

I'm just a bully that nobody likes,
I'm horrid and vicious and sad.
When others notice the things that I do,
That makes me very glad.

No one else behaves like me.
That's how I know I'm strong.
I hit and punch and steal their lunch
And snigger all day long.

They told me I'd be sorry,
I really can't see why.
To get some friends? Some mates like these?
Guess what? I'd rather die!

Liam, age 10

There are many important questions that link self-esteem and bullying: for example Is a child's self-esteem affected by bullying? What is self-esteem, anyway, and how can it be enhanced? What are the key influences on children's self-esteem? And can it be too high (see the verse written by Liam, a 10-year-old, as part of a drama activity).

Children with positive self-esteem believe they can succeed in what they wish to do, and they have the confidence to follow their dreams. They may choose a narrow focus or prefer a broader spectrum of activities and experiences, but they will have the self-belief that underlies success. This gives a psychological or attitudinal advantage as they look forward to meeting new challenges rather than fearing or avoiding them, and they see obstacles as things that can be overcome rather than hurdles that will defeat them. It helps them to be resilient and to bounce back quickly when times are tough. Positive self-esteem can also sustain children who are naturally lower achievers in an academic sense. It helps them keep their difficulties in proportion and saves them from being overwhelmed by negative evaluations. 'I know I can get there even if it takes a little longer . . . and I have other skills' is a wonderfully sustaining philosophy. It is based on high self-esteem.

It can be seen, then, that children who develop high self-esteem more easily achieve competence. And because all the different aspects of development (social, intellectual motor and emotional) interweave, positive self-esteem is pervasive across different skills. It boosts communication, motivation and perseverance across the board and so plays a significant and long-lasting role in both living and learning. It minimises fear of rejection and helps prevent self-blame, perhaps the most injurious kind of all.

The most significant part of being bullied in my view is the negative effect this has on the children's self-esteem. Those who are picked on – the victims – often believe they are at fault, and if this harassment continues, they may take on the mantle ascribed by the bullies and begin to believe they are worthless. The next step may be to worry about the effect this has on their families. As explained by 9-year-old Darren:

> When I admitted I was being bullied, my Mum was so upset.
> I could see she was nearly crying. I knew I had let her down and
> she had enough worries without supporting me. I should be able
> to stick up for myself but I'm hopeless.

The worst-case scenario can be that children take drugs to blot out the pain, even committing suicide as depression takes over and the future seems devoid of hope. Unfortunately, reassurances by parents can be less effective than negative comments from the peer group at this age because the relative placing of 'significant others' – that is, those who influence the child's beliefs – changes from family to the peer group in childhood. This is why friendships are so important.

But why should some children be outgoing, confident and demonstrative while others are withdrawn or aggressive, dwarfed by self-doubt? Is there a physiological and/or psychological reason why should be so? Johnson (1991) suggests that children's personalities should be seen as a see-saw or a split between dark and light. This follows from Jung's (1955) thesis that each of us has a 'living shadow' that holds all the negative components of the personality, or the things the person has no wish to be, for example deceitful, aggressive or proud. If the see-saw is tilted by experiences and reactions from others, then positive happenings should allow the light to emerge and subjugate the dark side. This is why school professionals readily give praise and report home using only positive comments. Unfortunately, the reality is more complex than the rhetoric, otherwise parents and practitioners would find it easier to prevent the dark side of children's personalities emerging. They would be able to prevent the emergence and dominance of 'deficit thinking' (McCarthy 2005) that emanates from the darker side of the personality. Perhaps when the negative shadow is most active, bullying behaviour, especially sadistic bullying, is the result? This would seem a feasible hypothesis. However, Valencia (1997) warns that these 'ascribed needs and deficits are always derived by imputation i.e. by observation rather than by scientific empirical research'. Even interesting and seemingly plausible theories have to be considered with caution. So, could bullying be further explained by addressing children's physiological make-up?

Carter (2000) offers both an explanation and a strategy through analysing happiness. This is important in the study of children who are victims or bullies or both, because it is likely that none of these children are happy. She defines happiness as the positive ethos resulting from the interaction of physical pleasure, meaning and the absence of negative emotion, and she explains that this state is caused by 'a rush of dopamine in the reward system of the brain'. The sensation of happiness, however, lasts only as long as the neurotransmitter dopamine continues to flow. As soon as the negative emotions generated by the amygdala, such as fear, anger or sadness, enter the equation, happiness is reduced. And the way to keep the amygdala low-key and stop it inhibiting happiness is to involve the body in work, preferably in non-emotional tasks. This is why hard work can dispel the blues.

However, a further required source of brain activity is required to ensure a sense of all-pervading well-being. For the world to be seen as a welcoming, meaningful place, the ventromedial cortex creates a feeling of cohesiveness; 'without it the world seems pointless and fragmentary' (Carter 2000). If this region does not function well, the result is depression. So, there may be complex neurobiological reasons why children who are bullies or victims do not listen to reason and fail to alter their behaviour to suit the parents' or professionals' pleas.

But despite these different inherent propensities, somehow parents and practitioners have to help all children to develop positive self-esteem. So the key question is, 'How can we make those who see themselves as sparrows believe they can be peacocks?'

The first step is to understand how the self-esteem is formed and the interactions that are most likely to boost it. Recognising the complexities can help explain why just telling children that they are good, clever, handsome or pretty when they know perfectly well they are not – or at least, they do not recognise themselves as such – does not always work. Boosting confidence needs ongoing positive support by someone the children regard as being significant – their ideal figure, if you like. Because of the vagaries of growing up, this may not be the people who love them best.

Understanding the self-concept and self-esteem

Self-esteem is one part of the self-concept; that is, the picture children build of themselves as they grow. The self-concept is a global picture and in the early years it tends to concern physical features, such as 'I am big (or small)', 'I have fair hair and blue eyes'. But gradually this picture enlarges to take in abilities and skills and characteristics gleaned from experiences in meeting others or hearing comments about prowess. So, descriptions such as 'I am clever' or 'good at sports' – whatever personal features children notice about themselves – enter the list. This picture expands as the children grow, but it is non-judgemental. The self-evaluation part (that is, 'I am better at sports than at sums' or 'I am a kinder person than my friend' or 'I can't do the things I want to do well enough – I'm a failure') is a judgement or assessment affecting self-esteem. This component develops gradually throughout childhood and adolescence and is dependent on the perception of the children; that is, how they view their status in conjunction with the experiences they have had and the value they place on them.

So, being naturally good at football might give a child who is interested in sports a huge boost and leave her more bookish but equally skilled friend unmotivated to practise and enhance her gift. For that child, adult comments on her sporting skills leave the child relatively unmoved. They contribute only marginally to her self-esteem. Important too is whether the child has a 'hero' and tries to emulate this person's attributes. The child's perceptions of his own possibility in reaching the goals set out by this 'ideal self' also impact on the formation of self-esteem. If the child sees these as attainable, even if the adult deems them unrealistic, then the child is encouraged, but if the gap between the child's self-judgement and the prowess of his hero is felt to be unbridgeable, then, particularly in sensitive children, motivation is affected, and in some, despair and depression can kick in.

It is interesting to note that children are not born with either high or low self-esteem. It builds as they grow and is formed by the reactions of significant others in the child's community, most usually parents, then teachers, then friends, and back to parents again! Self-esteem is not set in stone. Particularly in the early years, it fluctuates as different environments and experiences provide positive or negative feedback. It is exquisitely vulnerable to negative feelings at times of illness, change or stress, and signs that these evaluations have made an impact have to be recognised and ameliorated before they become fixed. Some of those signs may be children

- regressing to an earlier, more comforting era, such as engaging in thumb sucking, or using a comfort blanket after that stage has passed;
- wanting to spend time alone;
- being reluctant to speak about school;
- feigning illness;
- being offhand and/or aggressive;
- bed wetting, dreaming, not wanting to sleep alone.

When a child's self-esteem has taken a knock, that child might be described as 'having lost confidence in their ability to do' or as 'having a change of attitude to learning', for example in becoming less motivated to pay attention or finish a task. This can happen right across the spectrum of ability. There are a myriad of explanations why this might be so, but being bullied is a common one. This emphasises why such changes must be investigated rather than being accepted at face value – for a child who starts off with positive self-esteem can have that quickly destroyed by bullying tactics, especially if they persist and if the bully appears to get away with the aggressive or taunting behaviour. It is even worse if the bully appears to the victim to be a popular member of the peer group, for then the victims are sure they are to blame. This can engender complex and long-lasting feelings of anomie ('I don't fit in here') or hopelessness ('It's no use telling someone because that will only make things worse'). Somehow, adults must convince children that the ripples associated with 'telling' are not going to happen and take steps to see that they don't.

Helping each child to have positive self-esteem is not easy, for the children are unique products of a complex interaction of genetic effects – what they have inherited – and their environment – where they have been brought up. They will inherit their body build, and their self-esteem will be modified by how pleased they are with that and how it impacts on what they can do. They also inherit a number of temperament traits and these will determine whether they are naturally resilient or more vulnerable to the experiences they meet, even to the effect of the hurts that bullying brings.

Temperamental traits

Children are born with temperamental traits – in a biological model these would be called emotional reactivates – and they are carried in the genes. This explains why personality characteristics can be resistant to change. It is interesting to note that identical twins, even those brought up separately, have marked similarities in the temperaments they display (Bee 1999). This confirms the genetic influence on behaviour, though no researcher would deny that environment plays a very significant part in shaping temperament too. This kind of change is learned rather than innate. It allows children to adapt to the circumstances in which they find themselves and their perceptions of what kind of behaviour they wish, or are advised, to display. These traits – and as yet there is no agreement on the definitive group – may be placed on a continuum and they can explain why children brought up in the same environment can react so differently to what would appear to be the same events. Some temperamental spectrums could be:

Resilient		Vulnerable
Extravert		Introvert
Exuberant		Passive
Impulsive		Reflective
Enthusiastic		Reluctant

And there are many more polar constructs. Perhaps practitioners could reflect on children they know well and devise their own.

To avoid huge lists, researchers have attempted to collate them into like groups. Buss and Plomin (1986) suggest only three dimensions, namely *emotionality*, *activity* and *sociability*, and these have been widely used to assess temperament in infants and young children. Similarly, Thomas and Chess have clustered their early (1977) group of nine dimensions into just three that they name the *easy child*, the *difficult child* and the *slow-to-warm-up child*. I expect that practitioners will empathise with these descriptors and be able to allocate their children to each of these categories. The question as to whether these characteristics stay the same in different social situations is an intriguing one.

I find the first dimension in my own list particularly interesting! This concerns resilience and vulnerability. Bee (2004) explains that in the same situation – even in a severely disadvantaged one – the resilient child will see the positives and come up smiling. This may be because they have 'protective factors' such as a high IQ or secure attachments that buttress them from the stresses that defeat the vulnerable ones. On the other hand, the vulnerable ones will focus on the downsides and dwell on the hurts and disadvantages that accost them. In extreme cases this can lead to illness and depression. But even in everyday events at home or at school, the resilient children will be able to shrug off happenings that give anguish to the vulnerable ones. The environment (families, practitioners and those in the community) must recognise and take steps to particularly support the vulnerable ones and consistently and constantly show them that when something is half empty it is also half full.

Environmental influences

Environmentally their self-esteem is affected by cultural mores such as the family setting, such as where they live and who they stay with, the beliefs and practices they learn there and how these match or differ from those adopted by school. All of these influence the children's personal input; that is, what they see as important and how this affects their motivation and purpose in complying with or rejecting the learning experiences that are offered in school. From all of these sources the children build an internal model, meaning a picture of what they are and what they would like to be (that is, their self-image). The children's self-esteem is the distance between their self-image and their ideal self; that is the attributes they attribute to their 'heroes'. If practitioners are to be able to nurture the children's self-esteem, they need to understand all of this. That is, they need to know the children at a deep level; they need to know what has contributed to the children's self-knowledge and what has caused it to fluctuate – in common parlance, what makes each one tick!

These are the reasons why nurturing the children's self-esteem is so vital to their well-being. Positive self-esteem gives children confidence in their abilities and helps them:

- to recognise, accept and value the competences they have;
- to build a picture of what they can strive for (remembering that motivated children can surprise adults by what they achieve);
- to recognise and respect the competences or learning differences that others show;
- to make friends with other children and support those who are less able;
- to approach new challenges positively;
- to share and cooperate;
- to be resilient when things go wrong.

These are fundamental competences that become more and more important as the children mature and become more independent. On the other hand, low self-esteem is likely to cause the children:

- to become afraid of attempting anything new;
- to become resentful that others are ahead;
- to become frustrated and possibly aggressive;
- to sustain inappropriate ways of interacting;
- to disregard learning altogether;
- to be rejected and to join other rejected children;
- to be bullied or to become bullies themselves.

This scenario, which over time can escalate, must be avoided for the sake of the children themselves and all who grow and develop with them.

Body image

Another important component of the self-concept (the picture) that also affects self-esteem (the evaluation) is the body image, and, sadly, even very young children can compare their body image to their ideal, find themselves wanting and take inordinate steps, such as dieting inappropriately, to change. Glamorous images portrayed in the media endorse feelings of inadequacy, and while the children with high self-esteem can recognise the artificiality of what they see, or know they are too young to look like that, or shrug off the effects of knowing they fall short of this ideal, those with low self-esteem have their confidence in themselves knocked and negatively reinforced when efforts to change are not met with (instant) success. Again the children's perceptions may not be true, but adults' entreaties can fall on deaf ears. Youngsters who develop anorexia and, despite visual evidence to the contrary, see themselves as fat are extreme examples of this.

Does this mean that children have to be clever or slim and pretty or strongly built and muscular if they are to have positive self-esteem? Of course not. But again the answer is more complex than would first appear. Children have different standards and different priorities in what they see as important. Very often, practitioners can be surprised by the 'success' of children who have only modest intellectual abilities. Dowling (2004) points out that 'they may be blessed with "emotional stamina" that allows them to have insights into the lives of others and a highly developed level of empathy'. So their strengths are in building relationships with others. They have charisma or leadership qualities that are recognised but difficult to describe. Robert Gagné is a key educationalist who has placed 'leadership' in his list of indicators of giftedness. Hopefully, that will let it become a vital, recorded part of school assessment. This in itself could show the bullies what qualities should be valued and urge them to change their behaviour.

Again the issue may be clouded by children's wishes to be 'the same'. These can even override pride in the competences they wish to have. So, while some very clever children take steps such as getting sums wrong that they could perfectly well do, so that they appear to be the same as their peers, those with difficulties, unable to make any change, often despair because they see the gap between themselves and 'the desired state' as unbridgeable. To try to raise their image in the eyes of the peer group they may resort to being the class clown and be encouraged in that behaviour by others who, at the end of the day, still reject them as friends. Alternatively, they may become aggressive or withdrawn.

Yet there are many within these groups, such as gifted children or those with special needs, who, despite teasing, have the confidence to be themselves and stand up for the things they believe in. They refuse to change. Why can they resist the pressure? Perhaps the children's temperament is important here.

How does the support children receive at home give them the confidence to be themselves? A no-win scenario arises if parents attempt to bribe their children to do better or in a bullying scenario to 'stand up for themselves', for then the children's views of themselves as inadequate are confirmed. Alternatively, some parents, intending to offer comfort, may explain, 'you don't have to do well – we didn't'. Unfortunately, the child may resent these low expectations ('is that all you think I can do?') or accept them and give up trying altogether.

So, what can be done beyond understanding (because understanding is useful only when it prompts action)? That is, what can practitioners do to support the bully and the victim in terms of raising their self-esteem?

A reminder from Thornton (2007) that '27 per cent of children report being the victim of sustained hostility that made their lives a misery over weeks and months' is one stimulus for gathering ideas on what can be done. She advocates that the first move is to 'reform not only the victim but the bully' and also, in settings, 'to establish an environment where telling someone about bullying seems the normal and safe thing to do'.

Reforming the victim

Byrne (2003) suggests that there are two key factors that must be addressed when seeking to change the status of a victim. These are (1) vulnerability, and (2) reaction. Typically, victims are passive children who accept what is being done to them, and, sadly, this passivity or vulnerability is the very thing that ensures the bullying will happen again. Bound by the misery that engulfs them, they do not think out strategies that could improve their lot, such as seeking help from adults or other children. Possibly this is because they are afraid of their reaction or they rationalise that they will be labelled as someone who cannot cope. At the very least, contacting adults means victims have to admit being bullied, and this is a very hard thing to do. But if the bullying is to stop, then the victim must find or be helped to find ways to stand up for him- or herself.

As the bully does not expect a reaction from the victim, a first strategy to try is simply for the victim to shout, 'Stop'. This is not easy for a vulnerable child, but research has shown that it can be effective. While this surprise element may only temporarily halt the bully, it draws attention to what is going on and gives practitioners or other children a chance to intervene. It makes the bullying public rather than hidden away, and, given that many bullies fear their deeds becoming known to staff and the more responsible pupils who would report what they saw, this strategy could show that the victim was prepared to make a stand.

Most victims are isolates. It is the lack of a friend or support group that makes them vulnerable. Sadly, practitioners asking other children to 'let them play' is at best a temporary solution. A more promising approach is to find what the victim likes to do and to set up that activity, encouraging another child with similar interests to join in. 'It is the activity rather than the personality that counts in young children's friendships' (Bee 1999), because then they have something to share and to discuss. And once children have reliable friends, they begin to see their world in a calmer, less frightening light.

If friendships do not emerge, adults need to discuss with the victims ways of helping them develop their social skills. Perhaps they are showing their unhappiness by scowling and non-bullying children are being intimidated or being made to feel tentative about approaching. Because they are anticipating being bullied, perhaps the victim's body language is saying, 'Keep away'?

Using a mirror can have dramatic effects in helping children to recognise facial expressions and body language. This idea can develop into games, say with one child suggesting emotional expressions and another displaying them. Children can also be encouraged to look up (making them appear more confident) and even to say out loud, 'I can do this.' Developing mantras in the classroom, such as 'today we will look out for each other and be kind' and, with the younger ones, 'no one can say you can't play' can also show the kind of ambience and behaviour that will be approved.

Developing assertiveness

Byrne (2003) places much emphasis on victims developing assertiveness. 'The reaction to negative behaviour will be crucial in determining whether it will be repeated. Almost everyone will be tested, but not everyone will be bullied.' He knows that bullies thrive in a situation where their negative behaviour goes unchallenged. He uses the mirror to allow victims to see how drooped shoulders and cast-down eyes send out messages such as 'I am vulnerable', and urges the victims to develop assertiveness. He asks victims to 'pick out the bully who harms you most, stand firm, get your head and shoulders up and briefly look at the person and show the expression, "I don't like the way you behave."' If the victims doubt they can do this, staff are asked to role-play the scenario giving the children the chance to work on their body language. This opportunity to build a pupil–teacher relationship should also let victims know they are supported as they try to change.

Gathering a group of timid children together is another idea, for then solidarity in numbers comes into force. At the very least, the children find they are not alone, so being bullied cannot be their fault. (This may need to be spelled out.) At best they will develop the confidence to share their experiences and discuss ways to outwit the bully. But of course if the culture of the school is such that the individual or the group can approach staff knowing that they will listen and support them, that bullying incidents will be reported and not tolerated, then confidence in the system leads to competence in being strong.

Reforming the bully

At the root of the actions and interventions must be the belief that children who bully should not be seen as 'enemies', for non-verbal cues may communicate to them that there are too many hurdles to effect change.

Many bullies lack sufficient empathy to allow them to understand the effect of their actions. They need to be made aware of this lack and supported in realising the detrimental effects for them ('If you continue to make people unhappy, no one will like YOU') as well as their victims. They need to have an alternative way of behaving spelled out if they cannot visualise one for themselves. Often they underestimate the effect they are having on other children and they can be shocked by realising that words such as aggressive, even abusive, could be applied to them. They need practitioners to spell out the victims' feelings and understand their anguish. Moreover, once other non-bullied children recognise the pain that is being caused, they are less likely to join the bully or ignore unacceptable behaviour.

Staff have to try to understand why a child has become a bully and why, despite class activities and private discussions, that child persists in using damaging behaviour. Are the children in the lower academic groups and are they striving to gain status? Teachers then have to find ways to enhance the bully's self-esteem by giving praise in the areas where the child genuinely deserves it. Perhaps curriculum areas could be devised so that the child has the opportunity to shine? Or could the bully be given responsibility for looking out for younger children in the playground (under the eye of the playground supervisor, of course); that is, using the 'setting a thief to catch a thief' idea. This can really help, especially if the other children do not see the bully as being rewarded despite the bullying tactics that were employed.

And of course children must believe that the goals teachers set to improve things are achievable, whether they be social goals (such as 'can you work together quietly and happily for ten minutes?') or academic ones. These need to be framed in the light of each child's capabilities. Contracts of good behaviour and withdrawal of privileges are also possible strategies that should be tried, but bullies should know that unacceptable incidents are recorded as evidence; that there is a clear set of procedures for referral and that these will be put in place.

The responsibilities of pupils who witness bullying

Staff have to insist that if pupils witness bullying of any kind, they feed back the information about who was involved and when and where the incident occurred. The pupils have to realise that they are not telling tales but are behaving responsibly. Even knowing this may make the bullies reconsider their actions. Moreover, this is the first step in setting a culture of safety.

Trapped by reputation

Pupils who have bullied can find they are cast into a role that they would prefer to jettison but they are unsure how to do this. Sometimes other pupils will point the finger because in the past they have been at fault. Some may even falsely accuse or goad the child into unacceptable behaviour to cause a scene. When the teacher suspects this, then calm interviews showing respect, such as asking for the bully's interpretation of events first, and away from the accusers, can show that a fair hearing can sort things out. Remember that it may be as hard for the bully to prove innocence as for the onlookers to prove guilt.

But sometimes, despite everyone's best efforts, there may be no improvement, or even deterioration, in the behaviour. Then the school policy on bullying comes into force. The bullies will have been reminded of the stages over the duration of the campaign to have a positive change in behaviour:

1. If you have hurt another child, you will be warned to stop.
2. If bullying continues, your parents will be informed.
3. A further incident may lead to suspension.

Some schools now have an anti-bullying week, and this chapter closes with examples of the work of children in Pentland Primary School in Edinburgh.

Are you a bully?

Have you ever bullied anyone? What made you do it and how were you feeling at the time? If you do sometimes, what else could you do to feel good about yourself? People don't like bullies. You like people being nice to you so you should be nice to them.

Why do people bully?

There are a lot of reasons why some people bully.

-Bullies think they are tough and cool when they bully, they also think they are in charge.

-Some bullies are being bullied themselves.

-One of the biggest reasons people bully is because they are jealous.

-Some bullies may not even understand how wrong their behaviour is and how it makes the person being bullied feel.

-Some bullies do it to get attention.

Why is bullying harmful?

Bullying is harmful because?

. It can make people feel sick in a way.

. They lose confidence and may not want to go to school.

. Bullying can make young people feel lonely, unhappy and frightened.

. It makes people feel unsafe.

By Karen Jeffrey P7H

What is Bullying ?

Bullying is when someone is annoying you and getting on your nerves constantly.

There are different types of bullying: physical, mental and cyber bullying.

Cyber bullying is when someone is bullying you through the computer, text message or any form of technology.

Physical bullying is when someone is bullying you by punching or kicking you.

Mental bullying is when someone is bullying you by calling you or your family names.

By Robyn & Chloe
Pentland Primary
P7h

What can you do if you're being bullied?

Just remember that you're not the problem, the bully is. Here are a couple of things that you can do if you're being bullied.

- Try and spend time with your friends, bullies are cowards and usually don't pick on people if they're in a group.

- Tell the bully to stop and just walk away, just ignore them, most of the time bullies just want attention.

- Tell an adult you trust or write a letter to them. Don't think that it's telling tales, it's not, you have a right to feel safe and secure and the adults can do something to get the bullying stopped.

- Spread the word, people will listen and make you feel safe.

If the bullying continues try calling 'ChildLine's bullying line on 0800 44 1111 its open from 3:30pm to 9:30pm And the people on the other end will talk to you and give you friendly advice.

Why are some people bullied?

Some young people are bullied for no particular reason, but sometimes it's because they are different in some way perhaps it's the colour of their skin, the way they talk, their size or name. Sometimes young people are bullied because they look like they won't stand up for themselves.

6 Ideas and strategies to stop bullying

Class mantra

Be strong, say you can do it,
Keep your chin up high.
There's nothing that you cannot do,
But first you have to try!

Geraldine, age 11

Class mantra

A class mantra often helps, especially if the children make it up, for example 'Everyone in this class looks out for each other.' 'Everyone is really important.' 'We don't need an anti-bullying week because none of us are bullies.' 'We are all different – hooray!'

Scoring goals

Children are asked to make their own goals and decide whether these have been achieved. If the children say they have made no progress, then this admission scores an own goal (or the ball goes over the back line) and the child can try again or choose another football. Alternatively, if one child is hampered by another, he or she is awarded a penalty. This can mean giving some extra time or having another football or goal to replace the original choice.

Resources: On the wall, draw a football goal. Each child cuts out a paper football and writes (or the practitioner scribes) a goal for today or this week, whatever is appropriate.

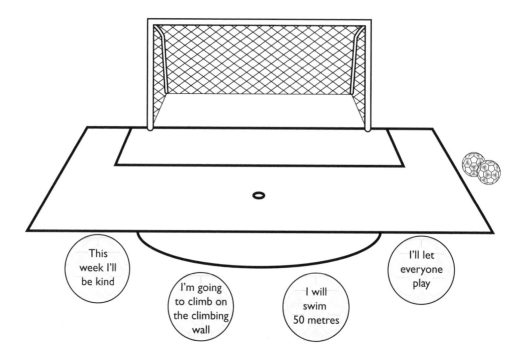

These goals are placed around the goalmouth. Then at the end of the day or week the children can decide whether they have achieved their goal (the ball goes into the net), whether they have not managed (the ball goes wide) or whether they tried and someone else prevented them achieving (they are awarded a penalty and have another turn).

Sample goals: it is good if the children can make up their own:

Today I will try fruit at snack time.
If someone takes my toy, I'll wait then ask for a turn.
I am going to wait quietly in line at lunchtime.
This week Tom and I will work together to finish our weather map.
I am going to thread beads for a necklace for Mother's Day.
I will try not to mix the paints but clean my brush first.
I will get my work done in time so that I don't have homework.
I will not chatter when the teacher is telling us about story writing.
I will not be so bossy.
I will let everyone join in.
When I feel unkind or angry I will count to ten and say something
    pleasant instead.

Alternatively, daily goals can be provided by the teacher and given to the children the night before so that they can think about how they might be achieved. The idea here is to provide each vulnerable child with one private target for the day ahead. The child can think about this the preceding evening, discuss it with his or her family and at the end of the day or at some quiet moment share thoughts on whether and how the target worked. This can work for the children who bully as well, with possibly different targets.

Bar charts

The children can be asked to make a bar chart or, for the older ones, a snakes-and-ladders board.

Bar charts can be introduced by collecting children's preferences concerning, for example, the things they like to play on in the park to the kinds of music or foods or treats they like. Then self-awareness items can be plotted in the same way.

Daily duties

Monday – Mark up the number of nice things you say to someone today. If you are unkind, you have to add a black mark. This could be done as a bar chart with different children using different colours.

Tuesday – Be ready with a phrase such as 'That's really boring' or 'You must be sad if you think I care.' Practise saying this as you look in a mirror. Make sure you look really strong.

Wednesday – Keep saying to yourself, 'I am strong.' Think back to something that upset you yesterday and talk with your parents or your teacher about what you did and perhaps some different ways you could have coped.

Thursday – Walk tall when you are in the playground – head up, shoulders back. Show that you are not afraid.

Friday – Share a poem with a friend, such as 'Two Little Kittens', 'The Giant' or 'The Kindly Giant'. What are the ideas that are behind the words in the poems?

**Poems and jingles containing ideas for discussions and drama
activities**

The Giant

There came a Giant to my door,
A Giant fierce and strong;
His step was heavy on the floor
His arms were metres long.

He scowled and frowned;
He shook the ground;
I trembled through and through.
At length I looked him in the face
And cried, 'Who cares for you?'

The mighty Giant, as I spoke,
Grew pale, and thin, and small,
And through his body, as 'twere smoke,
I saw the sunshine fall.

His blood-red eyes turned blue as skies.
He whispered soft and low
'Is this', I cried, with growing pride,
'Is this the mighty foe?'

He sank before my earnest face,
He vanished right away
And left no shadow in his place
Between me and the day.

Such giants come to strike us dumb,
But, weak in every part,
They melt before the strong man's eyes,
And fly the true of heart!

Charles Mackay

The Kindly Giant

There are giant footprints on the path outside,
a right one and a left one
make one great big stride.

But where is the giant? Where on earth is he?
I'm going to hide
where he can't see me!
Is he an ogre with eyes so harsh and grey?
If by chance he looks like that
we'll all run away!

Listen hard, I hear him coming down the lane.
Let's peep out and see him
then we'll hide again,
Did you see his big red nose and his merry twinkling eyes?
I'm sure he is a kindly giant;
what a nice surprise!

He's sitting in our garden saying, 'Please come and play,
I love to see young children,
they brighten up my day.'
And so we'll run to meet him and climb upon his knee
And ask him to tell us all
his history!

'When I was a little boy,' our kindly giant said,
'I lived up in the mountains
where the sky is red.
I tossed huge boulders down the mountainside
and swam the lakes
and made towns shake
and travelled far and wide.

'But now I'm older, it hurts me to see,
how lots of little children
are afraid of me.
So now I just keep smiling and do my best to show
that though I'm big, I'm just a kid
At heart you know.'

Christine Macintyre

Lessons from 'The Kindly Giant'

The key messages are that people can change and the benefits to be gained from being kind to others – that is, other people, not being afraid, will want to be friends. Children can act this out taking different parts, such as the giant, the villagers, the children. The children who are villagers act out, for example by whispering to each other, 'Have you heard the giant is coming? And the group discussion can introduce lots of new vocabulary such as 'fearful' ('let's all look fearful – is there anything that makes you feel like this – oooooh') and everyone pretends to shiver.

Children try out the giant footsteps; this is a good balance challenge! The younger ones can make footprints in the gunk tray; the older ones can draw round their prints and learn about the different parts (bones and ligaments) and, if appropriate, make graphs of shoe sizes in the group.

If one child takes the part of the giant stomping down the mountainside, others can dash in and out of hiding places quickly, showing their fear. Vocabulary can be extended; stomping, crashing, blundering or other ways of getting down a mountainside could be suggested, such as scree running, hang gliding, parachuting, hot air ballooning!

But then, when everyone sits down to listen to the giant, they discover he is friendly and smiling, so the discussion covers issues such as not jumping to conclusions from appearances – AND being prepared to give everyone a second chance!

The giant then reflects on the horrid things he did. The children love to 'throw boulders down the mountainside' and the discussion can ask them to imagine how the villagers feel. Again vocabulary can be enlarged. The older children can make pairs of words as opposites, such as

    big – small
    kindly – aggressive, horrid, noisy
    friendly – frightening
    merry – sad
    gentle – harsh

They could then think of situations where they themselves displayed these characteristics. Alternatively, discussions could cover notions such as 'If you have been unkind, what could you do to make it up to that person?' or 'What would you do if you met someone who looked grumpy?' or even, with the older ones, 'When you look back on your childhood like the giant did, will you be pleased, do you think?'

Once the giant's characteristics have been discussed, it is important to emphasise that with a little care and thought we can all change to be kinder people.

The following drawings are by Primary 1 at Longniddry Primary School.

I'm sticking my head out of the chimney. The giant is going to knock my house down with the boulder.

The glow-worm

This idea is intended for the nursery and Foundation Stage or primary 1 and 2.

'Here is a new friend come to live with us for a while. What kind of person do we want him to be?' (Draw a glow-worm or make one from a long scarf filled with old tights, sew-on eyes and a smiling mouth. Knit him a coloured hat. Ask the children to name him, then gather the children's ideas about where he should live, where he has come from and whether he is fully grown, etc.

A student teacher had great success trying this with 5-year-olds. They called their glow-worm Booker and offered the following suggestions:

> We want him to be good and not bite us.
> He has to be quiet because we are working hard.
> I hope he's funny and plays tricks – that would be good.
> We could ask him what he likes to eat and buy that food.
> Maybe he'll fight with Teddy in the corner?
> He looks angry – we could shut him outside.
> Is he a stranger? I'm not allowed to speak to him if he is!

This idea can lead to language development – practitioners gently adding words such as 'considerate', 'aggressive', 'naughty', and the children decide what characteristics are best. Able children can carry out research into glow-worms, or whatever the visitor is. In the class that tried this, the glow-worm became a real part of the class – he was given a birthday and the children made him gifts. He lived in the library corner and each day the children were anxious to find what book he had chosen to read when they were asleep. They loved it when Booker's choice matched their own. (The teacher can make sure Booker chooses the same book as a timid child.) One mother, believing Booker was a new boy in the class, actually wrote him an invitation to her son's birthday party!

Some days Booker was naughty and cross, and the children discussed how this made them feel, why Booker behaved like this and what they could do to make him feel better. Imaginative scenarios, such as Booker going out to play and another worm being unkind, could lead to discussions of the best ways to tackle bullying in the playground.

A page to help discussions on facial expressions

HAPPY

SAD

HURT

ANGRY

FRIGHTENED

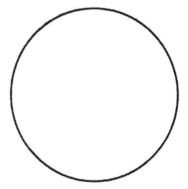

MAKE A FACE HERE

Two Little Kittens

Two little kittens, one stormy night,
Began to quarrel, and then to fight;
One had a toy, the other had none,
And that is how the quarrel began.

'I'll have that toy,' said the bigger cat;
'You'll have my toy? We'll see about that!'
'I will have that toy,' said the tortoiseshell
And spitting and scratching on her sister she fell.

I told you before 'twas a stormy night
When these two kittens began to fight;
An old woman took the sweeping broom
And swept them both right out of the room.

So they lay and shivered beside the door
Till the old woman finished sweeping the floor.

And then they crept in, quiet as mice,
All wet with snow, and cold as ice,
They found it much better, that stormy night,
To sit by the fire than to quarrel and fight!

Jane Taylor

This poem shows how silly it is to waste time quarrelling. It shows that when people squabble, there are no winners!

Fine Feathers

Peacocks have fine feathers,
But listen to their cry,
They strut and preen
Aim to be seen,
They certainly are not shy.

But listen to the skylark
Who sings a lovely song
He just has dowdy feathers
But enchants us all day long.

Christine Macintyre

This jingle asks children to look beyond the obvious and think of gifts different people have. It also makes them realise that shy children may be hiding their gifts and they need to be encouraged to show them.

This could precede the worksheets 'Who am I?' because it would suggest to the self-effacing children that they have hidden gifts they could share. Children could then list the talents in the class or gather a list of talents children would like to have.

Quips

Victims should understand they are trying to take the wind out of the bullies' sails!

- 'STOP' – If victims call out 'STOP' as soon as the bullies begin, then it draws attention to where the bully is and lets others intervene. This simple technique has been surprisingly successful.
- 'Go away. Stop bullying. You don't worry me. You must be so sad if you can't think of nicer things to do.'
- Sometimes the element of surprise can result from the victim seeming to agree with the bully – with a sting in the tail!

> 'You told me I was dumb and fat,
> I answered, "Yes, that's true,
> You told me so just yesterday,
> So I'm the same as you!
>
> "If that's all you can think of
> It really goes to show
> That mice have got into your brain.
> That's something we all know!" '

The following pages offer a selection of page-sized ideas for photo-copying.

For me ... About me

There are no correct answers – be honest. From this list circle some words that describe how you feel most of the time.

Happy	Worried	Friendly	Thinking I'll do well	Kind
Enjoying my day	Miserable		Down in the dumps	Looking forward to new activities
Aggressive	Dreading changes		Calmer not flustered	Jealous
Pleased to be me	Wishing I was someone else		I have lots of friends	I like to work on my own

Make a list of things
you are pleased with

Make a list of things
you would like to change

If someone else read this would they recognise you? Can you think how you are going to make the changes – how can you make your wish list come true?

Alien

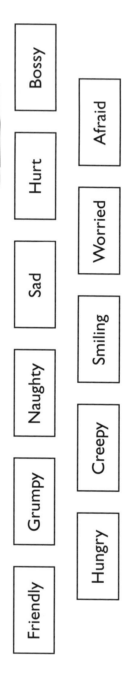

An alien comes into your playground. What do you hope he will be?

Colour the box you like best.

| Friendly | Grumpy | Naughty | Sad | Hurt | Bossy |

| Hungry | Creepy | Smiling | Worried | Afraid |

1 What would you do if he was friendly?
2 What would you do if he was afraid?
3 What would you do if he was creepy?

1) What makes you feel friendly? ....
           angry? ....
           sad? ....
           hurt? ....

Draw a friendly alien bringing presents from his homeland. What could they be?

Secret diary

Date 1) Date 2) Fill this in today. Hide it away then complete it again in two weeks. Are there any changes? What caused these?

	Yes	No	Sometimes
I have to answer questions quickly			
I get all my books/pens ready in time			
I listen carefully during lessons			
I daydream a lot of the time			
I get on well with the others in the class			
I find it difficult to sit still and concentrate			
I am kind to everyone I meet			
I am confident in asking questions if I don't understand			
I really enjoy playing with friends			
I always let people who want to be my friend come and play			
I bully children I don't like			
Some children bully me			
The teacher bullies me			

Choose one or two things you would like to change.
Work out how you are going to do this.

Date 2: Did you manage?

About ME!

I am usually …

	Yes	No		Yes	No
Happy	☐	☐	Friendly	☐	☐
Chatty	☐	☐	Too noisy	☐	☐
Sporty	☐	☐	A little bit lazy	☐	☐
Serious	☐	☐	Funny	☐	☐
Honest	☐	☐	A fibber	☐	☐
Have lots of good ideas	☐	☐	Grumpy	☐	☐

Think about how other people see you.

Do you want to change anything?   Yes ☐   No ☐

Draw or write about something that

a) makes you happy

b) makes you cross

Appendix

De Bono's six thinking hats

White

Focuses on information, e.g. 'What does the story tell us?' 'What is the problem that we have to solve?'

Yellow

A sunny positive hat. 'What are the good things, the benefits and values?'

Red

Feelings and emotions – 'How does that make you feel?' or 'In the story how did (the character) feel?'

Black

A careful, cautious hat – 'What difficulties might we find?'

Blue

A controlling hat – cool but concerned with the control of the other hats

Green

A creative hat – 'What else could we do?' 'What other ways could we try?'

From: *Bullying and Young Children*, Routledge © Christine Macintyre 2009

Bibliography

Ainsworth, M.D.S. (1973) The development of mother–infant attachment. In B.M. Caldwell and H.N. Ricciutti (eds) *Review of Child Development Research*, vol 3. Chicago: University of Chicago Press.

Ainsworth, M.D.S., Blehar, M., Waters, E. and Wall, S. (1978) *Patterns of Attachment*. Hillsdale, NJ: Lawrence Erlbaum.

Alexander, L., Currie, C. and Mellor, A. (2004a) Social context of bullying behaviours. HBSC Briefing Paper 9. Published by the Anti-Bullying Network, University of Edinburgh.

Alexander, L., Currie, C. and Mellor, A. (2004b) Bullying: health, well-being and risk behaviours. HBSC Briefing Paper 10. Published by the Anti-Bullying Network, University of Edinburgh.

Allergy Awareness Group (2007) Childcare environment: food allergies. Paper presented at Ickworth Hall Conference on Childhood Concerns, April.

Barrett, S., Prior, M. and Manjiviona, J. (2004) Children on the borderlands of autism, *Autism: The International Journal of Research and Practice* 8 (1): 61–87.

Baumrind, D. (1972) Socialization and instrumental competence in young children. In *The Young Child: Reviews of Research* 2: 202–224.

Bee, H. (1999) *The Growing Child*. London: Addison-Wesley.

Bee, H. (2004) *Lifespan Development*. New York: HarperCollins.

Bellhouse, B., Johnston, G. and Fuller, A. (2005) *Empathy: Promoting resilience and emotional intelligence for young people aged 7–11*. London: Paul Chapman.

Bond, L., Carlin, J.B., Thomas, L., Rubin, K. and Patton, G. (2001) Does bullying cause emotional problems? *BMJ* 323: 480–4.

Borstein, M.H. (1989) *Maternal Responsiveness: Characteristics and Consequences*. San Francisco: Jossey-Bass.

Borup, I. and Holstein, B. (2007) Schoolchildren who are victims of bullying report benefit from health dialogues with the school health nurse, *Health Education Journal* 66 (1): 58–67.

Buckley, S. (2007) *The Sue Buckley Research Fund Booklet*. Southsea, UK: Down Syndrome Educational Trust.

Buss, A.H. and Plomin, R. (1986) *Temperament: Early Developing Personality Traits*. Hillsdale, NJ: Lawrence Erlbaum.

Byrne, B. (2003) Countering bullying behaviour: a proactive approach. Paper presented at Galway Education Centre, March.

Carter, R. (2000) *Mapping the Mind*. London: Phoenix.

City of Edinburgh Council (2006) *Guidance on Positively Challenging Bullying, Racism and Discrimination*. Edinburgh: Children and Families Department.

Collins, M. (2005) *It's OK to Be Sad*. London: Paul Chapman.

Davies, A.M. (2002) Sound therapy through The Listening Program, *Patoss Bulletin*, May.

de Bono, E. (1999) *Six Thinking Hats*. London: Penguin Books.

Department of Education (An Roinn Oideachais) (1993) *Guidelines on countering Bullying Behaviour in Schools*. Dublin: The Stationery Office.

Dowling, M. (2004) *Young Children's Personal, Social and Emotional Development*. London. Paul Chapman.

Due, P., Holstein, J.L., Diderichsen, F., Nic Gabhain, S., Scheidt, P. and Currie, C. (2005) Bullying and symptoms among school-aged children: international comparative cross sectional study in 28 countries. *European Journal of Public Health* 15 (2): 128–32.

Eisenberg, N. (1992) *The Caring Child*, Cambridge, MA: Harvard University Press.

Eisenberg, N. (2002) *Altruistic Emotion, Cognition, and Behavior*. Hillsdale, NJ: Lawrence Erlbaum.

Harris, P. (1992) *Children and Emotion* Oxford: Blackwell.

Hartup, W.W. (1996a) The company they keep: friendships and their developmental significance, *Child Development* 67: 1–13.

Hetherington, E.M. (1999) Coping with family transitions: winners, losers and survivors. *Child Development* 60: 1–14.

Johnson, R.A. (1991) *Owning Your Own Shadow: Understanding the Dark Side of the Psyche*. New York: Faber & Faber.

Jung, C.G. (1955) *The Interpretation of Nature and the Psyche*. New York: Pantheon.

Keen, D. and Ward, S. (2004) Autistic spectrum disorder: a child population profile, *Autism: The International Journal of Research and Practice* 8 (1): 39–48.

Lewis, C. (1986) *Becoming a Father*. Milton Keynes: Open University Press.

McCarthy, J. (2005) The persistence and invasiveness of deficit thinking, *Learn: Journal of the Irish Learning Support Association* 27: P33–46.

Macdonald, K. (1992) Warmth as a developmental construct, *Child Development* 63: 753–73.

Macintyre, C. (2008) *Dyspraxia in the Early Years*, 2nd ed. London: David Fulton.

Macintyre, C. and Deponio, P. (2003) *Identifying and Supporting Children with Specific Learning Difficulties: Looking beyond the Label to Assess the Whole Child*. London: RoutledgeFalmer.

Mackay, C. (1933) 'The Giant', in *Excelsior Readers Book 11*. Edinburgh: Oliver & Boyd.

Moore, C. (2004) *George and Sam*. London: Viking.

Murray, M. and Keane, C. (1998) *The ABC of Bullying*. Dublin: Mercier Press.

Myers, B.J. (1984) Mother–infant bonding: the status of this critical-period hypothesis, *Developmental Review* 4: 240–74.

Nation, M., Vieno, A., Perkins, D. and Santinello, M. (2008) Bullying in school and adolescent sense of empowerment: an analysis of relationships with parents, friends, and teachers, *Journal of Community and Applied Social Psychology* 18(3): 211–32.

Neihart, M. (2003) Gifted children with attention deficit hyperactivity disorder, *ERIC EC Digest* 649.

Olweus, D. (1993) *Bullying at School: What We Know and What We Can Do.* Oxford: Blackwell.

Olweus, D. (1995) Bullying and peer abuse at school: facts and intervention. *Current Directions in Psychological Science* 4: 196–200.

Oppenheim, D., Sagi, A. and Lamb, M.E. (1988) Infant–adult attachments on the kibbutz and their relation to socioemotional development four years later. *Developmental Psychology* 24: 427–33.

Palmer, S. (2006) *Toxic Childhood*. London: Orion.

Parten, M.B. (1932) Social participation among pre-school children. *Journal of Abnormal and Social Psychology* 27: 243–69.

Peer, L. (2004) Otitis media: a new diagnosis in dyslexia? Paper presented at the BDA International Conference, University of Warwick, March.

Piaget, J. (1954) *The Construction of Reality in the Child*. New York: Basic Books.

Taylor, J. (1933) 'Two Little Kittens', in *Excelsior Readers Book 11*. Edinburgh: Oliver & Boyd.

Thomas, A. and Chess, S. (1977) *Temperament and Development*. New York: Brunner/Mazel.

Thomson, L. and Lowson, T. (2002) *Self-esteem 1*. Colchester, UK: Claire Publications.

Thornton, S. (2007) Bullying: A fixable problem? *Child Care* (London: Step Forward Publishing), November.

Todd, J., Currie, C., Mellor, A., Johnstone, M. and Cowie, M. (2004) Bullying and fighting among schoolchildren in Scotland: age and gender patterns, trends and cross national comparisons. HBSC Briefing Paper 8, University of Edinburgh.

Valencia, R.R. (1997) *The Evolution of Deficit Thinking: Educational Thought and Practice*. London: Falmer Press.

Winston, R. (2004) *The Human Mind*. London: Bantam Books.

Index